CAMBRIDGE LIBRARY COLLECTION

Books of enduring scholarly value

British and Irish History, Nineteenth Century

This series comprises contemporary or near-contemporary accounts of the political, economic and social history of the British Isles during the nineteenth century. It includes material on international diplomacy and trade, labour relations and the women's movement, developments in education and social welfare, religious emancipation, the justice system, and special events including the Great Exhibition of 1851.

The Exposition of 1851

Charles Babbage (1791–1871), one of the most original thinkers of the nineteenth century, is best remembered as the pioneer of computing technology, but he also made significant contributions to mathematics, mechanical engineering, philosophy and political economy. This book, first published in 1851, is an example of his active and effective campaigning for the role of scientists and the place of science, technology and technical education in society. Ahead of his time, Babbage was critical of government and the scientific community for not valuing science and technology in education. The work develops these themes, using the Great Exhibition as a backdrop to highlight the political and cultural factors that can impede scientific and technological progress. Britain's industrial supremacy, he argued, disguised the need to develop technical education. As relevant and persuasive today as in 1851, Babbage's arguments emphasise the fundamental importance of technology to the advancement of society.

T0304203

Cambridge University Press has long been a pioneer in the reissuing of out-of-print titles from its own backlist, producing digital reprints of books that are still sought after by scholars and students but could not be reprinted economically using traditional technology. The Cambridge Library Collection extends this activity to a wider range of books which are still of importance to researchers and professionals, either for the source material they contain, or as landmarks in the history of their academic discipline.

Drawing from the world-renowned collections in the Cambridge University Library and other partner libraries, and guided by the advice of experts in each subject area, Cambridge University Press is using state-of-the-art scanning machines in its own Printing House to capture the content of each book selected for inclusion. The files are processed to give a consistently clear, crisp image, and the books finished to the high quality standard for which the Press is recognised around the world. The latest print-on-demand technology ensures that the books will remain available indefinitely, and that orders for single or multiple copies can quickly be supplied.

The Cambridge Library Collection brings back to life books of enduring scholarly value (including out-of-copyright works originally issued by other publishers) across a wide range of disciplines in the humanities and social sciences and in science and technology.

The Exposition of 1851

Or, Views of the Industry, the Science,
and the Government, of England

CHARLES BABBAGE

CAMBRIDGE
UNIVERSITY PRESS

CAMBRIDGE UNIVERSITY PRESS

Cambridge, New York, Melbourne, Madrid, Cape Town,
Singapore, São Paolo, Delhi, Mexico City

Published in the United States of America by Cambridge University Press, New York

www.cambridge.org
Information on this title: www.cambridge.org/9781108052535

© in this compilation Cambridge University Press 2013

This edition first published 1851
This digitally printed version 2013

ISBN 978-1-108-05253-5 Paperback

THE EXPOSITION

OF

1851.

LONDON :
R. CLAY, PRINTER, BREAD STREET HILL.

THE EXPOSITION

OF

1851;

OR,

VIEWS OF THE INDUSTRY,

THE SCIENCE, AND THE GOVERNMENT,

OF ENGLAND.

BY

CHARLES BABBAGE, ESQ.

CORRESPONDING MEMBER OF THE ACADEMY OF MORAL SCIENCES
OF THE INSTITUTE OF FRANCE.

SECOND EDITION, WITH ADDITIONS.

LONDON:

JOHN MURRAY, ALBEMARLE STREET.

1851.

PREFACE

TO THE FIRST EDITION.

ENGLAND has invited the civilized world to meet in its great commercial centre; asking it, in friendly rivalry, to display for the common advantage of all, those objects which each country derives from the gifts of nature, and on which it confers additional utility by processes of industrial art.

This invitation, universally accepted, will bring from every quarter a multitude of people greater than has yet assembled in any western city: these welcome visitors will enjoy more time and opportunity for observation than has ever been afforded on any previous occasion. The statesman and the philosopher, the manufacturer and the merchant, and all enlightened observers of human nature, may avail themselves of the opportunity afforded by their visit to this Diorama of the Peaceful Arts, for taking a more correct view of the industry, the science, the institutions, and the government of this country. One object of these pages is, to suggest to such inquirers the agency of those deeper-seated and less obvious causes which can be detected only by lengthened observation, and to supply them with a key to explain many of the otherwise incomprehensible characteristics of England.

Who, for instance, could have conceived that England, after making unexampled efforts for the adoption of "*Free Trade*," should be the first nation to prohibit * its very basis, "*competition*," at the world's great bazaar?

This country is fortunate in having on the Western Continent, a great nation derived from the same common stock, speaking the same language, sharing the same feelings, but fortunately not partaking the same *prejudices*. Proud of the only ancestry which is not contemptible, it glories in the genius and the virtues of our common forefathers, and in its young ambition now strives in science and in literature, to prove itself *their* worthy descendants— *our own* generous rivals.

* See Chapter on Prices.

Separated from us by an intervening ocean, the judgment of America is not obscured by the repulsion or the fascination of personal manners,—by the tales of jealous rivals or enthusiastic friends. It can thus, as it were, anticipate for us the decision of posterity upon the reputation of those English writers who have never visited her shores. Many foreigners speaking other tongues, whose researches in industrial, economical, and physical science, have conferred honour on their own country, now visit ours. These and their congenial spirits throughout the world, sit in judgment on the *prejudices* of England, and will, if I mistake not, find ample reason to agree with the Danish statesman in the opinion,—that great nations are often governed by very small people.

England has invited the judgment of the world upon its *Arts* and its *Industry;*—science appeals to the same tribunal against its *ingratitude* and its *injustice.*

Several friends whose esteem I prize, have urged me to avoid everything personal,—some even to suppress this volume. I value their friendship, whilst I reject their counsel. In illustrating the

position of science in this country, it would have
been affectation not to have mentioned the Calculating Engines.   Who else *could* have fully known,
— who else *would* have fully told their history ?

It has been suggested to me that, to select
individual examples for illustration, is personality.
To have made general charges without them,
would have been termed *vague*, and would certainly
have been *useless*.   It still however appears to me
that a *single* illustration in each case, would cause the
least pain, and might yet be sufficient for the purpose.
If it is thought otherwise the remedy is easy.

The facts stated in the following pages are not
drawn from any violation of the confidences of
private society : those whose names are mentioned,
are paid by the nation, and therefore responsible to
their employers.   Against them I have no personal
feeling ; their official acts are necessarily mentioned
as parts of the system to which they belong.

The remark most frequently made has been, " that
the publication of this volume will do me injury."
This opinion is indeed a severer censure on the
conduct of the government than any I have myself
pronounced.   I do not agree in it, for I know of

no injury within the power of those who have never given me a single occasion for gratitude.

Bad men always hate those they have injured ;— Good or great men, when they have discovered that they have been unjust, always more than repair the injury they have committed.

Those who, from an acquaintance with the case, can truly interpret this volume, will *know* that I have abstained ; they will *see* that I possess the power, though not the disposition, to avenge injury. But the same spirit which has carried me through difficulties few have encountered, at the expense of sacrifices which I hope fewer may ever be called upon to make, forbids me tamely to submit to injustice.

The reader of these pages will observe that I have exposed with an unsparing pen the dishonesty of party. The modes employed by it to " discredit" and intimidate an honest man are various.

If he agree with them in a principle, but differ in its application, he is called " *crotchety.*" If he cannot be induced by sophistry to vote with them against his sense of right, he is called " *impracticable.*" If, when passed over in the appointment

to some office for which he is qualified by knowledge and entitled by position, he complain of the
neglect; notwithstanding he continues to vote with
his party, he is called a "*disappointed man.*" If,
however, he has energy, and is backed by great
political or professional interest, he may then secure
a *present* peerage for himself, his wife, or his
relative, with a promise of better treatment when
anything desirable becomes vacant.

At last, having discovered that his party are sincere and united only in their desire to retain office;
if his arguments admit of no refutation,—if his
perception of right can be obscured by no sophistry,
—if he can himself be cajoled by no flattery,
seduced by no advantage, deterred by no intimi-
dation, from expressing his real opinion upon the
merits of his party: then, although he may support them whenever they are true to their principles, yet he is pronounced a "*cantankerous
fellow.*" Thus bad names are coined by worse*
men to destroy honest people; as the madness of
innocent dogs arises from the cry of insanity raised
by their villanous pursuers.

* "A bad old woman making a worse will."—BYRON.

The merit of the original conception of the present Exposition is insignificant in comparison with that of the efforts by which it was carried out, and with the importance of its practical results.

To have seen from afar its effects on the improvement, the wealth, and the happiness of the people— to have seized the fit moment, when, by the right use of the influence of an exalted station, it was *possible* to overcome the deeply-rooted prejudices of the upper classes—to remove the still more formidable, because latent, impediments of party—generously to have undertaken great responsibility, and with indefatigable labour to have endeavoured to make the best out of the only materials at hand,— these are endowments of no ordinary kind.

To move in any rank of society an exception to its general rules, is a very difficult, and if accompanied by the consciousness of the situation, a very painful position to a reflecting mind.

Whatever may be the cause, whether exalted rank, unbounded wealth, surpassing beauty, or unrivalled wit,—the renown of daring deeds, the magic of a world-wide fame; to all within those narrow limits the dangers and the penalties are

great. Each exists an isolated spirit; each, unconsciously imprisoned within its crystal globe, per-
ceives the colours of all external objects modified
by those tints imparted to them by its own surrounding sphere. No change of view can teach
it to rectify this partial judgment; throughout its
earthward course the same undying rainbow
attends to the last its parent drop.

Rarely indeed can some deep-searching mind,
after long comparison, perceive the real colours of
those translucent shells which encompass kindred
spirits; and thus at length enable him to achrom-
atise the medium which surrounds his own. To
one who has thus rectified the " colour-blindness "
of his intellectual vision, how deep the sympathy he
feels for those still involved in that hopeless obscu-
rity from which he has himself escaped. None
can so justly appreciate that sense of loneliness,
that solitude of mind, which surrounds unquestioned
eminence on its lofty throne;—none, therefore, can
make so large an allowance for its errors;—none
so skilfully assist in guiding its hazardous career.

The triumph of the industrial arts will advance
the cause of civilization more rapidly than its

warmest advocates could have hoped, and contribute to the permanent prosperity and strength of the country, far more than the most splendid victories of successful war. The influences thus engendered, the arts thus developed, will long continue to shed their beneficent effects over countries more extensive than those which the sceptre of England rules.

———————

P.S.—The greater part of this Work was in type some time previous to the opening of the Exposition :—it would be of no interest to the public to explain the cause of this delay.

═══════

NOTE ADDED TO THE SECOND EDITION.

It has been suggested to me that, without some explanation, the Author of this Volume might appear to have reserved his opinions on the subject of the Exposition, until it was too late for the Commission to make use of them. This was not the case.

Being fully aware of the importance of such exhibitions, and having myself, many years before, endeavoured to connect them with the British Association, I hailed the announcement of the plan as one calculated to produce the most extensive good. At that period I was in Paris, and both abroad and at home I have uniformly spoken of the Exposition with the highest approbation.

On one or two points I differed entirely from the opinion of those to whom its management was confided. The questions of the *site of the building*, and of *affixing prices to articles exhibited*, were the most important of them. I took the earliest opportunity of expressing strongly my views on those subjects to several personal friends who were members of that Commission, nor did I ever fail to communicate through the fittest channel any circumstance I became acquainted with which might advance its interests.

CONTENTS.

CHAPTER I.

PAGE

INTRODUCTION 1

CHAPTER II.

ERROR RESPECTING THE INTERCHANGE OF COMMODITIES   7

CHAPTER III.

OF SOCIETIES 12

CHAPTER IV.

ORIGIN OF THE EXPOSITION OF 1851 26

CHAPTER V.

OBJECT AND USE OF THE EXPOSITION . . . 42

CHAPTER VI.

LIMITS 48

CHAPTER VII.

SITE AND CONSTRUCTION OF BUILDING . . . 55

CHAPTER VIII.

PRICES 64

CHAPTER IX.
PAGE
PRIZES 99

CHAPTER X.
JURIES, ETC. 112

CHAPTER XI.
ULTERIOR OBJECTS 125

CHAPTER XII.
INTRIGUES OF SCIENCE 149

CHAPTER XIII.
CALCULATING ENGINES 173

CHAPTER XIV.
POSITION OF SCIENCE 189

CHAPTER XV.
THE PRESS 202

CHAPTER XVI.
PARTY 209

CHAPTER XVII.
REWARDS OF MERIT 220

APPENDIX.
THE ELEVENTH CHAPTER OF MR. WELD'S HISTORY OF THE ROYAL SOCIETY 251

CHAPTER I.

INTRODUCTION.

ONE of the most frequent sources of mistaken views in economical science, arises from confounding the nature of *universal* with that of *general principles*.

§ *Universal principles,* such as the fact that every number ending with the figure five is itself divisible by five, rarely occur except in the exact sciences. Universal principles are those which do not admit of a single exception.

General principles are those which are much more frequently obeyed than violated. Thus it is generally true that *men will be governed by what they believe to be their interest.* Yet it is certainly true that many individuals will at times be governed by their passions, others by their caprice, others by entirely benevolent motives : but all these classes together, form so small a portion of mankind, that it would be unsafe in any inquiry to neglect the great principle of self-interest. Notwithstanding, however, all the exceptions we may meet with, it is impossible to take any just views of society without the admission of general principles, and on such grounds they will be used in these pages.

Self-interest, combined in various degrees with knowledge, assumes the most diversified forms. It excites our contempt or raises our admiration, according to the littleness or the greatness of the object it pursues—according to the temporary or the more distant advantages it seeks. On the one hand, it governs the minister of a party on his doubtful eminence, whilst on the other it guides the enlightened statesman to the object of his distant ambition.

§ Again, it is admitted as a general principle that *each man is the best judge of his own wants and of his own interest.* Now although many individuals, and even whole classes of society, have at times been thought by more enlightened men to have formed erroneous opinions as to their true interest, yet, when it is remembered, that every man must see many views of his own case, and must know many facts connected with it, which he has not communicated even to his most confidential adviser, those who have had most experience are most inclined to believe that the exceptions are much less frequent than at first sight would appear.

Another source of erroneous opinions arises from neglecting causes apparently insignificant.

In taking a comprehensive view of any subject, it is very desirable to throw into the shade all its minor points; but in estimating the consequences of any set of facts, there is another condition which must be fulfilled, before we can arrive at accurate conclusions. If we are about to neglect a cause on account of its apparent insignificance, it is *essential* that it should not be one of *frequent* recurrence. Thus, if a labourer inconsiderately lift his shovel but an inch or two more than is necessary to throw its load into his barrow, although the exertion of force is trivial in each instance, its repeated occurrence during the whole day, will produce at its conclusion a very sensible difference either in fatigue or in the amount of the work done. Napoleon is said to have remarked of Laplace, when he was Minister of the Interior, that he was too much occupied with considering *les infiniment petites*. To dwell upon small affairs which are isolated, is not the province of a statesman; but to integrate the effect of their constant recurrence is worthy of the greatest.

One of the most important processes in all inquiry, is to divide the subject to be considered into as many different questions as it will admit of, and then to examine each separately, or in other words to suppose that each single cause successively varies whilst all the others remain constant.

But this most obvious doctrine of common sense

has frequently been contested in questions of
economical science, and has been often character-
ized as theoretical, and as entirely inapplicable to the
affairs of life. It is certain that very little progress can be made in any subject without this aid,
and it is hopeless for those whose minds are
incapable of mastering the simpler questions, ever
to institute successfully an investigation into their
united action.

A familiar illustration will explain this better.
Two men are making an excavation, removing the
earth in the usual way with spades and wheelbarrows.

One of these men, Q., does more work than his
companion P., and if an inquiry is made, Why is
this so? the usual reply would be that Q. is either
stronger, more active, or more skilful than P.

Now it is the third of these qualifications which
is the most important, because if Q. were inferior
even both in strength and in activity, he might yet
by means of his skill perform a greater quantity
of work without fatigue.

He might have ascertained that a *given* weight of
earth raised at each shovelfull, together with a
certain number of shovelfulls per hour, would be
more advantageous for his strength than any other
such combination.

That a shovel of a certain weight, size, and form
would fatigue him less than those of a different
construction.

That if its handle were two or three inches longer than he required, its additional weight would at the end of the day have been uselessly lifted many hundred times.

That if each spadefull of earth were lifted but an inch or two above the barrow beyond what was necessary, a still greater waste of force would arise.

That if the barrow itself had its wheel at a distance beyond the centre of its load, it would be more fatiguing to draw.

That if the barrow had upright sides, it would require more exertion to turn out its load than if its sides were much inclined.

Thus although Q. might have less strength and less activity than P., he might yet by skill and practice, have arrived at some combination of these tools which should enable him with less fatigue to do more daily work than P.

But in order to have arrived at this degree of skill, Q. must when a boy have been taught to examine *separately* the consequences of any defect or inconvenience in the parts of the tools he was to use in after life, or in the modes of using them. If not so taught, he must have arrived at the same knowledge by the slower and more painful effort of his own reflections.

In either case he would be able to communicate his knowledge to his friends or his children; and if circumstances induced or obliged him to enter upon

a new trade, he would naturally apply those principles to his new tools.   Indeed, whatever subject
might be presented to a mind thus trained, such
habits of inquiry would most probably be applied
to its examination.   Thus, by the early education of
his reasoning faculties on the trade by which he is
to subsist, he would not only render his own labour
more productive, but would have his mind better
prepared for the reception of other truths.

CHAPTER II.

ERROR RESPECTING THE INTERCHANGE OF COMMODITIES.

THERE exists in society a widely-spread error relating to the very principle of that interchange of property between individuals which is usually called a bargain. It is almost always supposed that one party is a gainer whilst the other is a loser. Indeed, by those whose reasoning on the subject has been limited to this single view of the question, it is with some plausibility maintained, that since the quantity of the commodities interchanged is in no case augmented by the bargain, the gain of one party can be accomplished only by an equal loss on the part of the other.

The insufficiency of this reasoning depends upon the truth of the principle that each party, being the best judge of the pleasure or advantage he can derive from the possession of a thing, *himself* decides that in his own case it will be increased by the exchange.

It may, however, be asked, How does it happen

that the sum of two commodities so exchanged has a greater value after the exchange than before? or in other words, Whence has the profit arisen?—is there any third party at whose expense it has been acquired? The answer is—that there is another source which almost always either directly or indirectly contributes towards this profit. The advantage is most frequently won by industry and knowledge from nature herself.

§ The following illustration, which happens also to be a tolerable approach to truth, will explain this principle more clearly :—

It is found by experience that the upper-leather of Boots made in France, is better and more durable than the upper-leather manufactured in England. On the other hand, it is found that the leather prepared in England for the soles of boots is less permeable by water, and more durable than that made in France.

Let us suppose that in each country a pair of boots will endure twelve months' continual wear ; after which time they are thrown aside.

In England the destruction of the boots will arise from that of the upper-leather, whilst in France it will be caused by that of the sole. Let us also suppose that the upper-leather of France will wear three months longer than the French soles, and reciprocally that the soles of England will wear three months longer than the English upper-leather.

Under these circumstances, it is clear that if the inhabitants of each country insist on making their boots *entirely* with the produce of *their own* tanneries, the average duration of a pair of boots both in France and in England will be twelve months.

Let us assume, for the sake of simplicity, that in each country the upper-leather and the soles have the same value. Then it is equally clear, if England were to give to France a million pair of soles in exchange for a million pair of French upper-leathers, that one million of the inhabitants of each nation would find their boots last during fifteen instead of twelve months.

This prolonged duration of their boots would not have been acquired by any sacrifice on either side : the exchange is here for the common and great advantage of both.

This probably arises from the joint action of many causes. The animals which in each country supply the hides, may either from breed, from food, or from climate be best adapted to produce that kind of leather in which each country excels. The water, the bark, or the climate peculiar to each country, may then contribute its share to the same effect. Again, the industry, the skill, and the knowledge of the people employed, as well as the character of the population and the distribution of its capital, may also have its influence on these results.

If we pursue this illustration one stage further,

it will appear that it is our interest not only that we should make these exchanges with France, but that she should also make exchanges with other countries than our own.

Let us suppose that France, having a larger population than England, required for its annual consumption two million pair of boots, and also that she possessed no other commodities which we required. Under these circumstances there could be no further direct interchange of leather, and France would possess a million pair of upper-leathers beyond our demand. But it is clear that if France could exchange these upper-leathers for the wools or any other produce of Germany which we might require, she would not only gain the additional duration of three months for her own extra million pair of boots, but would also enrich us by the advantage which we should derive from the exchange of the strong hides of England for the produce transmitted to us from Germany.

§ The general result of all those inquiries of which only the slightest sketch has now been attempted, is that—*the free and unlimited exchange of commodities between nations, contributes to the advantage and the wealth of all;*—that this benefit arises from no sacrifice on the part of one nation for the profit of another; but that the sum of the productive powers of man is by these means, without any increased labour, largely augmented throughout the world;—that this increment is won partly by the suppression of ignorance and fraud, and partly by the united effects of industry, of skill, and of science, in compelling nature to minister to the wants of man.

All who admit the truth of these principles, must feel an earnest desire to support every effort which may assist in their dissemination amongst the masses of mankind. Education is the earliest, and the most effective aid ; but it must be secular education. It must be the education of the faculties of each child, with reference to the wants of his future course of life. The religion of the uneducated and unenlightened man, even when true, partakes of the nature of superstition, and instruction in religious truth *alone* will not be enough : his mind must be opened and informed on other subjects also. He who by observation and inquiry has arrived at the conviction that any line of conduct which is dishonest towards his neighbour, will most probably prove unprofitable to himself in this world, will surely have a strong additional motive to guard him in the hour of temptation from those courses which his religion teaches him will incur punishment in a future state.

CHAPTER III.

ASSOCIATIONS for occasional discussion, of men pursuing the same or similar studies, have long been found advantageous for the inter-communication of the difficulties, the doubts, and the discoveries of students. In more recent times, when each art has gradually connected itself with the sciences on which its success depends, the importance of these meetings has become obvious to the manufacturer, although in this country it may not yet have become apparent to the statesman.

The Academia del Cimento, the Royal Society of London and the Academy of Sciences at Paris, have had a long series of imitators in the principal cities of the civilized world. The increasing extension of science and the wants of its cultivators, have led them to subdivide their pursuits and to form Societies specially devoted to each separate subject.

§ These learned bodies, however, are of a stationary character, located for convenience in some capital or large city. With the advance of civilization new wants arose, and Professor Oken of Munich, feeling the great advantage of periodical meetings of the cultivators of the natural sciences, organized an annual assemblage of German naturalists to be held successively in each of the great cities of Germany, thus rendering the field of friendly intercourse and of scientific observation much more easily accessible to all who felt an interest in their common object.

Although the earliest meetings were small,* their value was soon perceived, and the cultivators of other sciences more or less connected with natural history, were gradually admitted, to the manifest advantage of all parties, until at the great meeting in 1828 at Berlin, the physical sciences themselves possessed their fair share of eminent representatives. But another important improvement had already commenced : foreigners were admitted to this German union, and amongst upwards of four hundred members, although nearly thirty were aliens in language and in country, they were welcomed with the warmest kindness by their enlightened friends.

Baron Alexander Humboldt, the President of the Association, in his inaugural address proclaimed its principle in the following words :—

" May those excellent persons, who, deterred

* The first was held at Leipsic in 1822.

" neither by the perils of the sea nor of the land,
" have hastened to our meeting from Sweden,
" from Norway, from Denmark, from Holland, from
" England, and from Poland, point out the way
" to other strangers in succeeding years, so that
" by turns every part of Germany may enjoy the
" effects of scientific communication with the differ-
" ent nations of Europe."

At that meeting a map of Europe was published
on which were conspicuously indicated those towns
and countries only, which had sent representatives
to this congress of intellect. On that map Austria
figured an intellectual desert, not because her philosophers were less industrious in the researches of
science, less acute in combining into laws the facts
they had ascertained, nor in any way unworthy of
sitting amongst the congregated talent of their own
or of other races : but because the government of
the country, more ignorant of its interest than the
philosophers were of theirs, refused them passports.

§ A few years afterwards, the light of truth
having penetrated official heads, the learned of
Europe, to the credit of the Austrian government,
were invited and hospitably entertained at Vienna.
The stability of the great empire which welcomed
them, was not shaken by their patient and acute
discussions : and it was at last perceived that unless
when depressed by neglect or persecution, philosophers possess in their own departments subjects

of far more animating and delightful interest than the unstable and inconclusive discussions of politics.

Sweden sent thirteen representatives to the meeting at Berlin in 1828, Denmark seven, Poland three, Holland two. Russia, France, England and Naples each sent one.

§ An account of this scientific congress at Berlin was published in 1829 in the *Edinburgh Journal of Science*. It was communicated by the author of these pages to Sir David Brewster. In the number of the same Journal for April, 1831, is an account by J. F. W. Johnstone, Esq., of the meeting of this scientific Congress, at Hamburgh, in September, 1830. Sir David Brewster, in conjunction with the late secretary of the Royal Society of Edinburgh, Sir J. Robison, and the Rev. William Vernon Harcourt, and several other cultivators of science, resolved on attempting to organize a similar institution in Great Britain. The difficulties as well as the advantages of this undertaking were then discussed. In Prussia the social position of men of science is quite different from that which they occupy in England. In Prussia the sovereign was aware of the value of science to his country, and was therefore induced to support it by an enlightened patriotism as well as by a generous ambition. In England science is pursued by no powerful profession which can aid or thwart the measures of the minister of the day. He is, therefore, indifferent to its progress, and is usually incapable of distinguishing the charlatan from the philosopher.

§ In 1831 the first meeting of the British Association for the Advancement of Science was held at York. It was proposed by those who undertook its management, that each succeeding meeting should be held in some large city or town at a considerable distance from that which received it in the previous year, and that after its objects had become well understood by the public, it should complete its cycle by holding a meeting in the metropolis. But it was soon felt that in order to influence public opinion, it was necessary that it should combine larger interests than were yet enlisted in its cause.

Such at that time was the state of education in England, that amongst the influential classes, country gentlemen, lawyers, members of parliament, peers, &c., few were found qualified for, or even capable of taking any interest in the then *existing* Sections of the British Association.

Accident fortunately supplied an occasion for remedying, at least partially, this defect. The opportunity occurred at the meeting at Cambridge in 1833, and was instantly seized upon, although in a somewhat irregular manner. Professor Quetelet had been deputed by the Belgian government to attend the third meeting of the British Association. The varied knowledge and enthusiastic love of

science possessed by M. Quetelet, might have qualified him to take part in any of its sections, but it
so happened that he had brought over with him
some highly interesting statistical documents which
unfortunately could find a reception in none.
Under these circumstances, a gentleman * who fully
understood their value invited a few of his private
friends most interested in that subject to meet
M. Quetelet in his own rooms in college, for the
purpose of talking over this valuable budget. The
author of these pages was one of those thus
honoured. He perceived the advantage that might
be taken of the accident, and immediately suggested
to his friend that the invitation should be extended
to all those known to be interested in statistical
inquiries, and that those present should at once
form themselves into a Statistical Section, and then
apply to the council for a bill of indemnity for the
irregularity. The plan being unanimously approved
of, it was immediately acted upon, and before the
termination of the meeting a Statistical Section was
not only recognised by the Association, but was
as fully attended as even the most popular of the
other sections.

At the concluding meeting of the Statistical
Section at Cambridge it was resolved, that a more
permanent body was necessary to carry out the

* The Rev. Richard Jones, Professor of Political Economy
at Haileybury.

views and wishes of the section, and it was agreed
to establish a Statistical Society in London.
The author of these pages was deputed to carry
out those arrangements which terminated in its
establishment.

The more pressing difficulty being thus removed,
the principle of extending the basis of the Association so as to unite the interests of various classes,
was steadily and unremittingly pursued. The
Physical and Mathematical Section was divided,
and a new section, that of the practical application
of mechanical science, or Civil Engineering, was
formed. The next step was very important, but
more difficult to accomplish. It was proposed by
an exhibition of the raw produce, the processes,
and the instruments for the production of manufactured goods, to unite in the same common
interest, not only all the consumers, but all those
who contributed to the production, or even to the
distribution of wealth.

The numerous foreigners who flocked to these
annual meetings of the British Association, might,
it was naturally thought, be induced to bring over
with them new instruments of science, or objects of
art and industry, the produce of their respective
countries. Whilst thus giving, and receiving in
return new ideas and valuable information, the
commercial interchanges between different nations
would necessarily be augmented by the steadily

increasing knowledge of the wants of each, and by the peaceful rivalry of all.

The first exhibition of this kind took place at Newcastle in 1838. The number of exhibitors was not large, but it was hoped that with time and encouragement this commencement might lead to much more extensive expositions of more general utility. It was followed by another on an enlarged scale, held at Birmingham in the succeeding year, after which it was discontinued.

The following extracts from a letter addressed by the Author to the Members of the British Association, were printed in 1839 :—

" My reasons for not resigning the trusteeship " of the British Association at Newcastle were, that " by retaining it until the following meeting, I " should give the Society more time to select my " successor ; and that by remaining on the council " until the meeting at Birmingham, I might be " enabled to assist more effectually in the arrange- " ment of the collections relating to the mechanical " arts, which it was anticipated would be amongst " the largest yet called forth by the British " Association."

" The real merits of the British Association " have been misunderstood by the superficial ; but " it possesses in its bearings upon the pecuniary " interests of large masses of the community a " power and an influence which nothing but great

" misconduct can destroy. Look at the manu-
" facturers of produce and of machinery, flocking
" to our annual meeting to interchange their ideas,
" enlightening their practical experience by the
" reasonings of science, and returning laden with
" the seeds of permanent ameliorations in their
" establishments. Look at the exhibitions of the
" productions of our factories, and say whether the
" humblest shopkeeper has not an interest in the
" existence of that body which gives publicity to
" the objects in which he deals, and which spreads
" them so largely before the eyes of those who can
" appreciate their merit, as well as of those who
" are likely to become consumers."

" These are material interests permanently en-
" gaged in our cause by the strongest ties—those
" of mutual advantage, cemented by reciprocity of
" kindly feelings."

§ This is not the place to discuss the causes
which have led to the present state of things. It
is sufficient here to observe, that if the views of
those who originally organized the British Association, had been supported both from within and
from without, in the manner which so important a
project in the history of science deserved, the
Exhibition of 1851 would have found itself led
by the science of the country, prepared by long
experience on a smaller scale, yet under very various
circumstances, to guide with some reasonable pro-

spect of success that gigantic undertaking, and to elicit from it the many invaluable services it might be expected to render to civilization.

Its legislative department would not have been committed to the guidance of a body of men, all of them respectable, and some, indeed, eminent in their several lines, but entirely inexperienced in the conduct and arrangement of any such undertaking —persons, all of them amiable and excellent in their private capacity, yet who have exhibited in their corporate union an entire ignorance of the great principle on which alone such expositions rest,—and who, contrary to the advice and the remonstrance of the best informed, have forbidden the most important quality by which men judge of commodities, their *Price*, from being attached to the objects on which their judgment is to be pronounced.

§ Long, however, before the origin of these itinerant societies, the voice of the statesmen of other countries, and the popular voice in England, had called into existence societies for the promotion of the arts connected with commerce and manufactures. In France, the " Conservatoire des Arts et Metiers" was established. In England the Society of Arts has endured above a century. Its novelty and utility caused it to flourish for a time : its seat in the metropolis of a people whose wealth and power arise entirely from the unbending energy

with which they apply themselves to advance the
arts and to extend commerce, added to its powers.
Yet, even with these advantages, that Society has
never risen to the position it deserved, and has
for years been languishing in premature decay.
Lately, indeed, a powerful impulse has been communicated to its proceedings, but even the pre-
sidency of the Prince-Consort has not yet raised it
to its due position in the public opinion.

The causes of this state of things are not remote.
The position of the Royal and of other societies
is equally influenced by them. Although intimately connected with the greatest interests of the
country, they can offer to those who give their time
or intellect to advance such objects, neither wealth
nor rank—neither place nor patronage. They constitute no distinct combination of men into a powerful class, like the Bar, the Navy, or the Army: they
are of no party, and finally, they are not fashionable.
It is true that the discoveries which such societies
profess to reward, are in many instances the source
of wealth to the few who, fortunately for themselves,
possess those other qualities necessary for its acquisition, but which are so rarely united with genius.
It is also true that wealth once acquired, will, if dis-
creetly employed, certainly lead its possessor to all
those other things, equally coveted as the great prizes
in the lottery of life by the Bar, the Military, and
even by the Church. Nor is this to be regretted,

seeing that the aristocracy of this country thus fortunately receives fresh blood and renewed intellect by adopting into its class the sagacious merchant, or the skilful fabricator of a princely fortune : the time may thus be postponed when the accident of birth will no longer be admitted as a fit qualification for a legislator. But even here it is the wealth of the aspirant that wins the position, not the integrity and sagacity of the man.

In France the government itself took the lead in directing an institution for the advancement of the arts. In 1795 it established the Conservatoire des Arts et Metiers, in which are deposited an extensive collection of drawings, models, and machines employed in the various manufactures of the nation.

Subsequently, ten professors were attached to this institution, to lecture gratuitously on those sciences more immediately connected with arts and manufactures. One of these devotes himself exclusively to the explanation of machinery in actual employment. There are also lectures on descriptive geometry, and on mechanical drawing. The expense of this establishment is about 6,000*l.* a-year.

§ The government of France perceived at a still earlier period the advantages which would result from the juxtaposition, at proper intervals of time, in one large building, of selected specimens of all the produce of the national industry, and in 1798 the first of these periodic meetings was held at the expense of the government. During upwards of half a century, at intervals of about five years, France, uninterrupted by the many changes in the form of its government, has continued to maintain these valuable expositions with increasing success and advantage. Prussia and Belgium also have adopted the plan of holding these meetings.

But if the principles on which they rest are well founded, it is clear that they are applicable to a still wider field : and that as in the Associations of science, cultivators from all nations are invited to be present, so in the Exhibition of the productions of industry the general advantage of mankind is most advanced by the joint contributions of the whole industrial world.

§ These views have long been felt and expressed, not merely by men of speculation, but by those who take a practical part in the affairs of life.

Enlightened French statesmen had long been aware of the advantage of this species of competition, and only abstained from proposing it until the conviction of the nation justified the foresight of its chiefs.

At length it was thought that the time had arrived for ascertaining more correctly the general opinion. Previously, therefore, to making the necessary arrangements for the Exposition at Paris in 1849, the Minister of Commerce sent circulars to the several Chambers of Commerce throughout

France, in order to ascertain whether it was the general opinion that foreign productions should be admitted to the competition.

The opinion of the public was not, however, sufficiently advanced to justify the undertaking; and considering the political situation of the country, the government wisely abstained from a measure which was not yet entirely in unison with the feelings of the people.

Thus it has happened that it was reserved for Great Britain, the country most interested in the cause, though the latest to adopt it, unprepared by any previous experience at once to attempt this vast enterprise.

CHAPTER IV.

ORIGIN OF THE EXPOSITION OF 1851.

§ It is not now necessary to inquire minutely into the origin of the present Exposition. It is sufficient to state that it appears to have been proposed by some members of the Society of Arts, who urged it on the attention of Prince Albert.

The magnitude of the undertaking, and the great principles on which it rested, seem not to have been fully understood, and the public were very imperfectly prepared either to appreciate its advantages or to contribute to its support. A capitalist was therefore sought, and found willing to undertake the risk of the speculation, and terms were agreed upon, by which £20,000 was advanced for distribution in prizes, one of which was to amount to £5,000. This contract contained some singular stipulations, and formed the basis of the proceedings for several months. It contained also a clause by which, on certain conditions, it might be cancelled within a limited time.

In order to carry out this undertaking, it was

proposed that a Royal Commission should be issued, over which, of course, Prince Albert should preside. As soon as these views became publicly known, they excited great discussion, and were the subject of much criticism.

§ The Ministers could not of course commit themselves by publicly avowing their disapprobation of an undertaking commenced under such high auspices. It might, however, readily have been foreseen that they would be averse to such a scheme, because whilst it was sure to give them a great deal of trouble, it would afford them no compensation in the shape of patronage.

Those, however, who usually reflect and retail the opinions of the Government, were by no means silent; at first it was said to be Utopian, then ridiculous, then, in the slang of official life, it was "*pooh-poohed*;" at a later period, when great public meetings had been held, and when public dinners began to give it an English character, the best speech which has yet been made on the subject, containing the far-sighted views of a statesman, was ridiculed as full of *German* notions, by coxcombs whose intellect was as defective as their foresight, and whose selfishness was more remarkable than either.

Another class of persons, the Belgravians, though actuated by the same motives, were induced to join in the outcry for other reasons.   As soon as it became known that the locality of the building would be the southern side of Hyde Park, they represented that the park would be destroyed, and become utterly useless. As if a building covering twenty acres out of above three hundred and twenty, could prevent the people from enjoying air and exercise on the remaining three hundred.

Again, it was asserted that by cutting down a few trees within the limits assigned to the building, the park would be desolated; the shady walks destroyed; whilst all the while there was a goodly stock of timber, old and young, abounding in the other three hundred acres. Before this absurd delusion could be removed from the public mind, all the plans were made specially to conform themselves to the enclosure of these miserable trees. It was not discovered until after the Crystal Palace was completed, that several of them were on the verge of extinction, and that all would probably perish by exposure under such unusual conditions. Some of the most decrepit and most inconveniently situated trees have now been cut down.

§ The Belgravians found out other causes of complaint. They could not tolerate the mass of plebeians of all nations who would traverse their sacred square, and they threatened to spoil the London season by going out of town. When it was suggested to them, that in these days of agricultural

distress, if they left town they might console themselves by letting their houses at a high price, they
refused to be consoled.

The Belgravians next consulted their " *medicine-
men*," who, seeing that they wanted to be frightened,
suggested to them that *some* foreigners were dirty,
—that dirt in *some* cases causes disease.   The Bel-
gravian mind immediately made the inference that
the foreigners would bring with them the plague;
then they dwelt on sanitary measures, and on the
danger to the public, until they themselves became
nearly insane.

It was then suggested that the foreigners might
become assassins by night,—or take military possession of London by day.   Their tradesmen too,
who hated the scheme, and knew the humour of
their customers, assured them that trade would be
entirely ruined; whilst at the same time, it was
whispered that many of them had sent large orders
to France for goods to be exhibited at the Crystal
Palace, and afterwards to be sold to their capricious
customers, either as French, or as English surpassing
French, just as the whim of the moment might
cause a demand for the one or the other.

This opposition of the inhabitants of Belgravia
increased as the preparations for the opening of the
Exposition advanced.   The working classes had
been favourable to the scheme from the commencement, and a knowledge of its advantages seems

to have advanced slowly in society from below upwards.

That the inhabitants of this fashionable quarter were necessarily exposed to some inconveniences cannot be denied. Their much-frequented riding ground was for a time interfered with, but they should have remembered that although the public at large *paid* for the maintenance of the park, the greatest portion of its advantages were *enjoyed* by those residing nearest to it.

Under these circumstances they ought to have been well content to forego for a time these trifling advantages, and to suffer with a good grace the little temporary inconveniences resulting from a plan which was unrivalled for the advancement of the arts of peace, and calculated not only to benefit our own country, but to contribute to the civilization of the world.

Notwithstanding much opposition and many prophecies of failure, a Royal Commission was at last appointed. It consisted almost exclusively of members of parliament, and of persons holding official situations. It was stated that not more than two of its members had ever seen a foreign exposition, and although it included many men distinguished in other departments of knowledge, there was scarcely one whose name was known to the nations we invited as at all eminent in that over which the Commission presided.

In England, a commissioner, however small his acquaintance with the subject, is always deemed fully competent in virtue of his appointment. The light in which this places us in the opinion of other nations is by no means flattering to our national vanity. It has been admirably described by an accomplished Italian resident amongst us in language which an Englishman might be proud to own, and with a degree of moral courage which few Englishmen would dare to exert on such a subject.*

It was easy to perceive that when so great a mass of people in distant quarters of the world was set in motion for such an object, it would be impossible to draw back, and that its own momentum would carry on the scheme.

§ That the Prince who took so strong an interest in it, and who saw so clearly and so far beyond the horizon which limited the view of those by whom he was surrounded, should become its chief, was quite natural. There are, however, circumstances in the state of society in this country, and in the constitution of human nature itself, which render it almost impossible to have unfettered discussion when a person of that exalted rank takes the chair at the meetings of a Committee.

* "What shall we do with the Glass Palace? By Spiridione Gambardella." London : Aylott & Jones, Paternoster-row.

The speech of the rash " commander of the Channel fleet" (page 9) is worthy of the pen of the celebrated wit who bestowed that appointment.

These objections are entirely unconnected with
the individual person, and if any amount of good
feeling and skill in such a Chairman could remove
the difficulty, we have fortunately had amongst us
several Princes who might easily have accomplished
it.   But the forms of society forbid in the presence
of princes that full and free discussion by which
alone the united knowledge of a Committee can
be brought into play.   Debates must take place
and divisions occur : otherwise some individual
may take upon himself to assume what either is,
or appears to him to be, the sense of the meeting :
this is much more frequently simply the expression
of *his own views*.   Thus, perhaps, he prevents the
statement of his opinion by some timid man, which
is possibly worth more than that of all the rest of
the Committee.

Again : in Committees presided over by persons
of this elevated rank, it is not an uncommon occurrence for some member, anxious for the success of
his *own* views, privately to hint in conversation with
other members, that these are the wishes of their
President.

To these objections, which are generally true,
there is, however, one exception.   When the Chairman is eminently conversant with the subject, while
at the same time the minds of the Committee are
like a sheet of blank paper,—the best course that
can then be pursued is to allow the Chairman to
interpret the sense of the Committee.

The first act of the Commission was most judicious.   It was to annul the contract with the
capitalist who had undertaken the building and the
commercial management of the Exhibition.   It is
to be regretted, however, that the actual amount of
compensation which he was to receive, was not
finally settled at the time.   The subsequent extent
of the undertaking having exceeded that which
was originally contemplated, may render this a
question of some difficulty.

The next step was to appeal to the public for
subscriptions to carry on the plan.   For this object
delegates were sent to many of the large towns,
some of whom, not possessing more knowledge of
the subject than the Commissioners themselves, and
having none of their tact, nearly caused the failure
of the whole scheme.

The knowledge and good sense, however, of the
working and manufacturing classes, supplied the
deficiencies of these missionaries, and the subject
became popular amongst them.   There were,
indeed, many exceptions even amongst these
classes.   Those whose business had been long
established, and who were manufacturing as largely
as their capital would admit, had no reason to seek
additional publicity for the sale of their produce.
Upon them the Exposition would impose only
trouble and expense, without any corresponding
advantage.

Others who possessed machinery of peculiar powers of production, or for the fabrication of curious products, were unwilling to expose these singular and costly machines to the eyes of their rivals from all countries. The produce of such machines being generally novelties, they found a ready sale for it, and therefore had no reason to seek the Exhibition as the means of publicity.

The extent of the demand for space at the Exhibition, has been as was naturally to be expected, so great, that it was quite unnecessary to press any person to exhibit who was not fully aware that it was for his own interest to do so.

With respect to the subscriptions, there are some observations which it may be useful to make for the sake of all subscribers to future schemes. It is said that the total amount subscribed is nearly 90,000*l*. of which only about 60,000*l*. have been paid.

No subscription ought ever to be advertised until it has been actually paid. It is quite unjustifiable to employ the money of *bonâ fide* subscribers in paying for advertisements to gratify the vanity of those, who are ambitious of appearing large donors, and who are yet so mean as to decline fulfilling their pledges.

This practice has, unfortunately, of late years been too prevalent. Persons of rank and position in the country have condescended to allow their names to appear in lists, for subscriptions which they never intended to pay, the effect of which has been to decoy others who trusted to their respectability and truth. The public in future will do well to abstain from subscribing to *any list*, however respectable the names may apparently be, unless it is distinctly stated that the subscriptions advertised have really been paid.

In the present case it would be a further waste of money to advertise the defaulters : but the Commission have a remedy, and they owe it to the genuine subscribers. Let a circular be sent to each defaulter, announcing that unless his subscription is paid by a certain day, his name will be returned to the clerk of the *Black list*, who has directions to make an alphabetical index of defaulters, several copies of which will be exposed to the public in various parts of the Crystal Palace during the whole time of the exhibition.

If public opinion were fully ripe for such a vast industrial undertaking, it ought to be entirely self-supporting. This seems to have been the opinion of the Commission, and with every wish to assist that object, and every desire to make allowances for the want of all past experience on the subject, a few remarks may be made which may promote the interests of some future Exposition, even though unavailing for the present.

The first question is necessarily the position of the building, and the facilities for access and egress.

As this question is discussed in Chapter VII., it is sufficient here to state, that the amount received from the admission of the public will very much depend upon this point. On the other hand, the difficulty and expense of conveying the things exhibited, will not be very different in different localities. This arises from the fact that if a package has to be taken from a boat, a ship, or a railway, and to be conveyed by cart to the locality at which it is to be exhibited, the expense and the danger of injury will be but very slightly increased, whether it is carted an additional quarter of a mile, or mile, or even a still greater distance.

Another very important question arises as to the price of admission to the Exhibition. There is no doubt, that if it were entirely free to the public, it would be almost entirely useless. Nor is it less certain that various prices ought to be charged on different days. The Commission seem to have made a very fair selection for the commencement of the experiment. Perhaps it would have been better to allow Saturday to be one of the cheapest days of admission, because in many workshops the journeymen leave their work at an earlier hour on that day : by the sacrifice of the half day's work, they would then be able to spend a considerable portion of the day in examining those objects in which they take an interest.

Perhaps on a future occasion some such scheme of admission as the following might be found most

productive. After the exceptional days at the commencement, occupying the first fortnight, the
admission might be charged thus :—

	May	June	July	Aug.	Sept.	Oct.
	s. d.	s. d,	s. d.	s. d.	s. d.	s. d.
Mon. . .	1 0	1 0	1 0	0 6	0 6	0 3
Tues.. . .	10 0	5 0	2 6	2 0	1 6	1 0
Wednes.. .	5 0	2 6	1 6	1 0	1 0	0 6
Thurs. . .	2 6	1 0	1 0	1 0	0 6	0 3
Frid. . . .	1 0	1 0	1 0	0 6	0 6	0 3
Sat. . . .	1 0	1 0	0 6	0 6	0 3	0 3

The principle of this scale is, that each week day
shall gradually diminish in actual price, but shall
always preserve its relative price. Thus Tuesday is
always the day of dearest admission, Wednesday of
the next dearest, whilst Saturday is always the day
of cheap admission. These periods might be distributed by weeks instead of months.

Whatever arrangement is made as to the price of
admission, it is of very great importance that the
number of visitors at the various prices should be
noted and recorded for future use. It will indeed
be unfortunate if knowledge so important for any
similar occasion, should not be registered on the
present.

For this purpose *every* entrance should have one
or more self-acting turnstiles registering the number
of those who pass through it. Not only the public
who pay, but the exhibitors and all who have free
admissions should be registered. At the end of

each hour, when the clock strikes, each gate-keeper should enter in a book the number indicated by his register. Such a collection of facts, extending over the whole time of the Exposition, would not only be invaluable for any future one, but would furnish materials for other important inquiries.

The general state of the weather, which of course would have a powerful influence, might be known from other registers : but it would be advisable that at the end of each day some-note were made of the general state of the weather at the Crystal Palace itself.

§ After the first of these Expositions it seems probable that their advantages will become so well known, that it may be quite possible to let out the stalls to exhibitors under certain conditions. Foreigners might still be admitted to exhibit without payment, because the expense of carriage would more than compensate for the rent.

Some stalls might be granted without rent by the Commissioners, the peculiar circumstances of each case having been considered. Again, other stalls, or at least other means of exhibition, might be accorded to those who contributed articles of actual use in the building ; as for example, a large striking clock, a steam-engine to drive the machinery or to supply the fountains.

Other means might be readily devised of increasing the receipts, giving at the same time increased convenience to the public. Thus, from the great extent of the building, and from the crowd, it may become difficult to pass easily from one part of the building to another. Now if the stalls were placed back to back along the centre of the great longitudinal avenues, a railway formed of wooden planks placed edgeways might be raised above the middle of them at a height of about eight feet, which would interfere but little with the stalls.

On this open railway cars mounted on wheels bound with india-rubber,* in order to avoid all noise, might travel at the rate of from one to two or perhaps three miles an hour. These cars might have luxurious cushions, and hold parties of different numbers. One line in a side aisle, the "express," might be devoted entirely to conveying passengers from one end to the other at the rate of three miles an hour, setting down at six or more intermediate stations: the payment might be one penny, or perhaps, on grand days, two or three pence. The other lines should take parties slowly along, so as to allow time to see the crowd below and the wonders of the exhibition, which might be rendered more distinct by means of opera glasses. Each trip might occupy twenty minutes or half an hour, and be charged threepence, sixpence, or a shilling, according to the price of admission on that

* Or the rails themselves might have grooves lined with vulcanized india-rubber.

day. By these means multitudes of ladies, children, and even of men, relieved from bodily fatigue, might be able to acquire knowledge or derive pleasure, which without these resources it would be impossible for them to enjoy.

It is probable that the light iron framing of such cars might be provided gratuitously by some exhibitors, and the spring cushions and ornamental drapery might be supplied by others, in consideration of the advertisement thus afforded of the purveyor's taste and skill.

The chariots of these railways should be drawn by means of a rope connected with the motive power.

If dumb railways are not thought expedient, small galleries at least might be made to which admission should be obtained by a small payment, so that those who wanted to traverse quickly from one part to another of the building, might thus, by avoiding the crowd, save time.

Umbrellas, and sticks, and great coats might be taken charge of by ticket on payment of one halfpenny. Also, any visitor might be allowed to deposit on his departure a bag containing his catalogue, note-book, or any articles which it might be inconvenient to him to take home with him each day, as is customary at the railway stations.

Other accommodations will suggest themselves, to be provided on the payment of a very small fee ; for example, soap and water and a clean towel may be very desirable to some visitors, especially to those who may examine the machinery.

It is probable that there may occasionally occur large crowds pressing for admittance. It may be worth while to consider whether in such cases an additional reserved entrance might not be opened, through which ladies and children, and men whom age or indisposition has deprived of the physical force requisite for encountering a crowd, might be allowed to pass on the farther payment, say of sixpence or a shilling.

If it were possible to have a similar reserved enclosure close to the building, in which carriages might remain on payment of a small fee, much inconvenience would be saved to some of the visitors, and some advantage would result to those who did not avail themselves of it, in consequence of the diminished line of carriages at the public entrances.

CHAPTER V.

The approaching Exposition is considered by many as a great and splendid show, calculated to give pleasure and excitement to hundreds of thousands of persons. Even in this sense it would be beneficial, for it is always important that the pleasures of the people should be productive of some advance in their tastes and information. But its great and paramount value depends on other causes. Its object may be most concisely expressed by stating that—

The Exposition is calculated to promote and increase the free interchange of raw materials and manufactured commodities between all the nations of the earth.

Its object is not the exclusive benefit of England, and if any such mistaken view is still entertained, it may without hesitation be stated that it would be impossible by any mode of management to accomplish so selfish an object.

It is the interest of every people, that all other

nations should advance in knowledge, in industrial skill, in taste, and in science.   The advances made in the two latter subjects acquire *permanent* exist- ence only through the *publicity* given to their enun- ciation and discussion.   Refining and elevating all by whom they are received, new principles in taste or in science, as soon as they are accepted as truths, become the universal property of mankind.

In whatever distant country any man devises means of diminishing the cost of production of the commodity he deals in, the following effects will result—

He will make larger profits than usual.

He will then diminish his price in order to get more customers.

His rivals in trade now find it necessary to undersell him in order to get back their customers.

Whilst this competition goes on, the price of the commodity falls, a larger consumption takes place and new purchasers will arise, which for a time checks the fall.

Ultimately, his rivals in the trade either remove their capital into other lines of business, or adopt the improved process.

In the mean time the first discoverer will, if a prudent and industrious man, have realized a con- siderable capital, for he will be fully aware that in the present state of science no monopoly can be permanent.   He will rather seek for a succession

of moderate improvements, which exciting no immediate inquiry or rivalry, shall increase the average
per centage of his profits, thus constantly keeping
his manufactory one, or at the utmost, only two
steps in advance of his competitors.

When in consequence of such an improvement,
a reduced price and an enlarged demand has arisen
in his own country, the manufacturer will naturally
make inquiries whether at this diminished price
other countries may not be induced to become
purchasers. If this is the case, the fact of their
free interchange with him proves that they can
acquire his commodity at a less cost than they can
themselves produce it.

But although the Exposition itself could not and
ought not to have been attempted for the sole
benefit of this country, it is almost certain that
England will reap the greatest share of its advantages. This will arise from the more extended
system of her commerce, and from the habits of
her people. The profits of the merchant, other
circumstances being equal, depend upon the amount
of his capital. Similarly, the knowledge brought
back by the traveller in foreign countries, or derived
from his observation in his own, will mainly depend
on the stock of information he carried with him to
give in exchange.

§ To arrive at those principles by which the
Exposition ought to be regulated, it becomes neces-

sary to examine the nature and extent of the interests involved.

In all interchanges there are three distinct parties concerned—

The Consumer,
The Middle-man,
The Producer.

The overwhelming superiority both in amount of capital and in the number of the first of these classes, the *Consumer*, is at once apparent, and ought throughout the inquiry to be steadily borne in mind. In fact, each individual of the other two classes is necessarily a member of the first; for all men are *consumers*, and as such their common bond of interest is to purchase every thing in the *cheapest* market.

§ The class *Producer* is equally indispensable for the purposes of exchange, but its number is much more limited. The interest of each individual producer is, that he should sell his *own* produce at as dear a price as possible, whilst he purchases that of all other producers as cheaply as he can.

The class *Producer*, therefore, is not only comparatively small, but has really a very divided interest, arising only from the difference between the personal and the class interest of the individual.

§ The class *Middle-man* is more extensive, comprising merchants, brokers, factors, wholesale and retail shopkeepers, hawkers, &c. The profits of this class are generally regarded by the public with some degree of suspicion. It is often thought that their profits are exorbitant. But in truth this is not frequently the case. The division of employments necessarily produces middle-men, and the public in the long run obtain the articles they require with more convenience and economy, and at a less fluctuating price, than it would be without such agency. But the number of intermediate agents in any commerce is itself subject to change, in different trades and at various times: it is quite possible that these changes may not have taken place with sufficient promptitude, and thus the public may have suffered for a time either by an excess or a defect in the number of middle-men.

The interests of middle-men are, individually, the same as those of consumers. As a class, the extension of commerce is for their advantage, because they are paid according to the amount of exchanges made. But they have also another and a very powerful interest. They fear that if the public were acquainted with the manufacturing price of articles, it would consider the difference between that and the selling price as a tax imposed by the middle-man upon the consumer. The middle-man therefore has a direct interest in preventing the public from arriving at a knowledge of the prices charged by the original manufacturer. It is also the interest of the middle-man that the manufacturer should not know the price at which his produce sells by retail: but, as it is in most cases impossible to prevent this, few attempts at concealment are made.

§ It appears, then, that the interests of these classes may be thus summed up—

Consumers, including every human being, have a strong interest in the freest competition as producing the lowest price.

Producers have an interest in selling their produce in the dearest market, and therefore claim free competition. But they have no advantage in selling it at the highest price: because a high price limits the extent of the sale. Their object is that the profit on each article, multiplied by the number sold, shall be the greatest possible.

Middle-men, although usually adverse to competition, have yet a direct interest in the amount sold.

CHAPTER VI.

LIMITS.

ONE of the great difficulties in exhibiting together samples of the produce and the industry of the world, must obviously be the magnitude and consequent expense of any building capable of containing such an exposition. In order to do this most effectively, and to secure the greatest amount of space for the primary object, it became necessary to lay down principles within the limits of which the objects exhibited should be confined. No real difficulty opposed the definition of this boundary, even if a liberal interpretation were admitted.

The Fine arts and the Industrial arts, although of the highest importance each to the other, are separated by a sufficiently definite line of demarcation, even at the points at which they most nearly approach. The characteristic of the fine arts is, that each example is an individual—the production of individual taste, and executed by individual hands; the produce of the fine arts is therefore necessarily costly. The characteristic of the industrial arts is, that each example is but one of a multitude,— generated according to the same law, by tools or machines, (in the largest sense of those terms,) and moved with unerring precision by the application of physical force. Their produce is consequently cheap.

The fine arts idealize nature by generalizing from its individual objects: the industrial arts realize identity by the unbounded use of the principle of copying.

The union of the two, enlarging vastly the utility of both, enables art to be appreciated and genius to be admired by millions whom its single productions would never reach; whilst the producer in return, elevated by the continual presence of the multiplied reproductions of the highest beauty, acquires a new source of pleasure, and feels his own mechanical art raised in his estimation by such an alliance.

§ This distinction between the fine arts and those of industry, would appear to place some of the latter in a class to which they are not yet generally admitted. It might seem that all lace not produced by machinery, must according to this view be admitted amongst the fine arts.

There are in the Exhibition some beautiful examples of such lace amongst the productions of other countries as well as of our own. They are made by the united labour of many women. The cost of a piece of lace will consist of—

1.—The remuneration to the artist who designs the pattern.

2.—The cost of the raw material.

3.—The cost of the labour of a large number of women working on it for many months.

Let us compare this with the cost of a piece of statuary, which is undoubtedly of a much higher class of art ; it will consist of :—

1.—The remuneration to the artist who makes the model.

2.—The cost of the raw material.

3.—The cost of labour by assistants in cutting the block to the pattern of the model.

4.—Finishing the statue by the artist himself.

In lace-making the skill of the artist is required only for the production of the first example. Every succeeding copy is made by mere labour : each copy may be considered as an *individual*, and will cost the same amount of time.

In sculpture the three first processes are quite analogous to those in lace-making. But the fourth process requires the taste and judgment of the artist. It is this which causes it to retain its rank amongst the fine arts, whilst lace-making must still be classed amongst the industrial.

Here we may observe the strong analogy which

unites these very different processes. If we continue the examination we shall find other resemblances, and by contrasting sculpture with lace made by machinery, we shall see in the very nature of their production, the wide interval which separates the industrial from the fine arts.

In the making both of lace and of statues, the remuneration to the artists can only be reduced by producing a larger number of them through more extended education. The expense of the raw material is small in both. The expense of labour in lace-making is very large, and it is perhaps considerable also in sculpture. The discovery of more convenient localities yielding marble, may make some diminution in its cost; and the improved manufacture of thread may slightly reduce the price of lace. A reduction in the price of labour may to a very moderate extent reduce the cost of the raw material of both. But it is evident that any *very great* reduction is not to be expected.

Let us now contrast this possible reduction with the past history of some industrial art. The plain lace made at Nottingham, called patent net, will supply us with a good example. In the year 1813 that lace was sold in the piece at the rate of 21s. a-yard. At the present time lace of the same kind, but of a better quality, is sold under the same circumstances at 3d. per yard. Thus, in less than forty years the price of the industrial produce has diminished to one eighty-fourth part of its original price.

§ The fine arts, already possessing a building and an exhibition of their own, which usually opens on the same day as that proposed for the opening of the Palace of Industry, it seems difficult at first to imagine why the limited space disposable within the latter edifice should be occupied by any portion of a subject exclusively belonging to the fine arts. Yet it has been decided that Sculpture shall be admitted but Painting rejected.*

Supposing both departments of art to be equally excluded, there would still be a propriety, and even almost a necessity to admit some examples of each. New tools used by the sculptor, suppose for preparing the block, might require an example of their mode of application; whilst the effects produced on the surface of the marble by other tools, could only be shown by comparative specimens.

Machinery of a very beautiful kind has been contrived for copying accurately, on a reduced or an enlarged scale, both medals and statues. The Venus de Medici itself could not be justly excluded from a purely industrial exhibition, — if

---

* Since this was written, the beautiful effect produced by sculpture in the Crystal Palace has fully justified the decision of the Commission. In fact, the only real objection to the admission either of sculpture or painting arises from the extent of space required.

placed in the centre of a series diminishing on the one side to a statuette of a foot high, and increasing on the other to a figure double her own height. Such a series, though fairly introduced as an illustration of industrial art, would, indeed, itself be highly interesting to the fine arts, as exhibiting the effect of change of magnitude, when the proportions remain identical.

Enamel painting would be excluded as belonging to the fine arts, but every painting on porcelain partakes in fact of the nature of an enamel painting. A service of porcelain would of course be admitted as a specimen of mechanical art, however highly it might be adorned by this form of painting.

New modes of engraving might be exhibited, analogous, for example, to that by which medals are so beautifully represented. There are several new methods of surface printing for multiplying original designs. In all such cases it would be very desirable to place before the eye of the spectator, the originals from which the copies were derived, and it might also add to the utility and interest of the Exposition, even to exhibit other forms of engraving of the same subject, for the sake of comparison.

The instruments by which daguerreotypes and talbotypes are produced, would assuredly claim a place ; so also might a collection of their results.

It would also be instructive that some of these productions should be accompanied by the original forms or paintings from which they were copied.

The general rule, therefore, might be, that specimens of the fine arts should not be admitted by themselves; but that they should not be excluded,— as illustrations,—either of the use of some tool or instrument by which their own production might be assisted,—or as forming parts or decorations of objects of the industrial arts,—or for the sake of comparison with the copies or imitations of them produced by these latter arts.

CHAPTER VII.

SITE AND CONSTRUCTION OF BUILDING.

THE questions connected with the construction of the building, were surrounded with considerable difficulties, even to the best informed. It should be capable of containing specimens, not merely of all the manufactured products of the world, but also of all the raw materials now used, and even of such, as being presented to the attention of competent persons, might probably become useful hereafter.

The site of such a building, its fitness for its purpose, and the cost of its construction, were the chief points to be considered.

Its situation especially was the most important, because that circumstance would greatly influence the number of persons visiting the Exposition, and therefore the amount of the receipts out of which the building was to be paid for.

The first principle which should guide the choice of a site, is obviously the *convenience of visitors;* and a little observation, or a moderate share of common sense, will show how the principle should be applied.

It is known to all those who have observed the course of crowds of human beings going to and returning from some centre of attraction, that if the spot on which the assemblage is to take place is subject to our choice, much of the difficulty of the arrangements will be removed.

Other circumstances being equal, that site is the best which admits of the greatest number of independent channels by which the multitude can arrive and retire. The means of access should be so arranged that various divisions of the visitors would, according to the quarter in which they reside, naturally take each its own most convenient course, without the necessity of any instruction from police or attendants.

Various sites had been proposed. Hyde Park;— the Regent's Park;—Primrose Hill, still more distant;—fields on the south side of the Thames intended to form Battersea Park.

It is fortunate that neither of the two latter was chosen, although they had many advocates: for in all probability the receipts would have been diminished by at least a third, if not by a half.

Various situations were pointed out in Hyde Park. One on the north nearly facing Hyde Park Gardens—one on the south nearly opposite the Barracks; this latter was ultimately chosen.

§ But a different position may be pointed out which combines so many advantages that it is much to be regretted it was not placed at the disposal of the Commission.

The distance between Cumberland Gate and the gate at Hyde Park Corner, is about 1,300 yards, or nearly three quarters of a mile. On the eastern side of the park, adjoining Park Lane, there is a narrow strip occupied by plantations, the circular reservoir and gardens.

On the open ground adjacent to this strip, but rather nearer to Cumberland Gate, the Crystal Palace might advantageously have been placed. Its length being nearly 629 yards, each end would have been about 350 yards from the two great roads of access. This site would have possessed the following advantages :—

> 1. Its distance from the north or south entrance of the park would, for the average of visitors, have been considerably less than that of the present site.
>
> To persons standing at Hyde Park Corner or at Cumberland Gate, the respective ends of the building would have appeared, from its great elevation, almost close to them.
>
> 2. There are very few trees upon it, and those few are still young.
>
> 3. It is the highest ground in the park, and could, therefore, be better drained.

In its present position the building can scarcely be seen from either of those positions. It is above

half a mile from Hyde Park Corner : whilst it is three
quarters of a mile by footpath, and nearly a mile and
a half by carriage drive from Cumberland Gate.

The large majority of visitors from the north and
the south will enter the park through these two ap-
proaches. The average distance, therefore, which
each will have to travel in the park, will be nearly
three quarters of a mile.

	Yards.
The distance of the nearest end of the present building from Hyde Park Corner is about	940
From Cumberland Gate is, by footpath, about	1560
Ditto, by carriage, about . . .	2490
The distance of the end of the proposed site from Hyde Park Corner, is about	375
Ditto, from Cumberland Gate . .	375

If we consider how many persons might have
entered close to a building thus placed, through
Grosvenor and Stanhope Gates, or through any temporary ones near them, it will be perceived that this
average distance would in fact be much diminished.

Supposing that an equal number of visitors arrive
by each approach, we have some means of approxi-
mating to one portion of the inconvenience and
loss which the public will suffer from its present
position.

In the first place the number of visitors has been variously estimated from one to seven millions. Let us suppose it to be four millions. Each of these four million visitors will, on an average, have to travel one mile and a quarter more than would have been necessary to go to and return from the Exposition. Thus five millions of miles will be uselessly traversed. If the expense of transport were one penny a-mile, and the value of time on an average four shillings a-day, the account would run thus—

$\qquad$ 2,000,000 persons travel $1\frac{1}{2}$ mile.
$\qquad$ 1,000,000
$\qquad$ 6)3,000,000 miles at six miles per hour.
$\qquad$ 10)500,000 hours.
$4s.=\frac{1}{5}l.$)50,000 days of ten hours each.
$\qquad$ 10,000l. value of lost time.

A similar calculation of the time lost by 2,000,000 persons travelling three miles an hour would give 13,333l.

The expense of travelling at 1d. per mile of the first 2,000,000, who travel in carriages, gives—

$\qquad$ 12)3,000,000 miles.
$\qquad$ 20)250,000
$\qquad$ 12,500l. cost of carr. of two millions $1\frac{1}{2}$ mile each.
$\qquad$ 10,000l. cost of time of ditto.
$\qquad$ 13,333l. cost of time of two millions at 1 mile each.
$\qquad$ 35,833l. total loss.

In this estimate the price of one penny a-mile may perhaps be thought high, especially when it is known that many will go on foot, others in omnibus, others in their own carriages : but in order to remain the same number of hours in the present building, from the extra time required to visit it, it will be necessary for many persons to spend one additional day in London, which could scarcely be done under twenty pence even by the poorest visitor.

The allowance of six miles an hour for travelling in omnibus or carriage, considering the stoppages of the one, and the crowd on the single road of approach for both, will be admitted to be moderate.

The rate of four shillings per day, or twenty-four shillings per week, as the value of the time of the visitors, will probably be thought less than its average value.

There can be no doubt that under these disadvantages the actual site must cause the loss of a large number of visitors, who would have partaken of the enjoyment in the more favourable position. The amount of *pure loss* thus suffered by the visitors as a class, must be withdrawn from the sum they intended to expend on their visit.

One of the earliest acts of the Commission was to advertise for plans of a building suitable for their purpose.

Certain principles were laid down. It should be *temporary* in its character—it should be econo-

mical in its cost—it should be fire-proof or nearly
so—it should be built and fit for use in an incon-
ceivably short time, and capable of being removed
in still less.

A lithographed plan of the ground assigned for
it, was circulated for the use of all who chose to
make suggestions, or to compete for the prizes
offered for the most approved designs; this insured
a certain amount of uniformity in scale, which rendered comparison easier. Although, from necessity, a very short time could be allowed for
preparation, yet 240 designs for the building were
offered.

These were exhibited to the public at the apart-
ments of the Society of Arts; a certain number of
them were selected as worthy of praise, and some
as deserving more substantial rewards.

There appears to have existed from the beginning
in the public mind, not only in England but on the
Continent, a belief that the Commissioners would
not be very rigid in interpreting their rules. This
was probably confirmed by the sudden and unlooked-for withdrawal of the large prizes that had
been promised to the public at the commencement.
Accordingly, the various plans seemed to vie with
each other in violating the rules laid down by the
Commission; those selected for reward were not
the most consistent with them. In order to give
confidence to the future, it would have been expe-

dient, previously to examining their merits, to have rejected all which grossly violated the conditions proposed by the Commission.

Beautiful plans might be suggested for magnificent buildings, if the designers were alike reckless of cost and of time of construction, and those who had honestly confined themselves to the prescribed conditions felt, with some reason, aggrieved at finding the violators of them applauded and rewarded.

Although there was, in the opinion of the Commissioners, much of beauty and genius, and many suggestions of value, yet none of the plans approached their own idea of what was requisite. It was therefore resolved that the Commission should itself originate one, availing themselves of the hints contained in these plans.

In the mean time, Mr. Paxton, who had devised and successfully carried out a new kind of architecture, the chief material of which was glass, came to their assistance. He drew the plans of his singular design, and was fortunate enough to find in Messrs. Fox and Henderson a firm capable of supplying all those mechanical details necessary for its success, and even of contracting to execute the work in a period of time so short that it will probably long remain unrivalled in the art of construction.

The Commission accepted this offer, and the present beautiful building arose as if by magic.

Amongst all the curious and singular products which the taste, the skill, the industry of the world, have confided to the judgment of England, there will be found within that crystal envelope, few whose manufacture can claim a higher share of our admiration than that palace itself, which shelters these splendid results of advanced civilization.

The building itself was regularly manufactured. Simple in its construction, and requiring the multiplied repetition of few parts, its fabrication was contrived with consummate skill.   The internal economy with which its parts were made and put together on the spot was itself a most instructive study.*

* The reader will find very interesting details and drawings of this manufacture in the "Illustrated London News," and in the " Expositor."

CHAPTER VIII.

THE great mass of consumers are always anxious to know the *price* of a commodity. To them it is the most essential consideration in a purchase. The thoughtless rich care little about the price, and those who don't intend to pay, care still less about it. The most knowing of this latter class, indeed, often deceive the vigilance of honest tradesmen by affecting a peculiar earnestness about cheapness. It is quite true that many well-known articles in great demand have a certain market price, and some a certain fixed price; as for instance, a penny roll. In this latter case the judgment of the purchaser is directed to its size, or its goodness, or to both those qualities together.

§ It may be useful to trace out the course of purchases by retail, and to show the fine gradations of impediment which are insensibly interposed between the vendor and consumer, as obstacles to a full examination of the article by the latter. Of course neither an article of daily consumption ought to be taken as an example, nor yet one immediately wanted by a consumer, whose time is so valuable that it would be cheaper to go into the first shop he finds and purchase it at any price.

§ Let us suppose that a lady having some leisure goes out in search of a fan. She passes several shops in which they may or may not be kept for sale.

She sees some fans in a shop window, but as they are *not open* she passes on, intending to return to them if she cannot suit herself elsewhere.

A few doors beyond there are some fans *open*, but none of them exactly suit her taste, and she does not like to give the owner of the shop the trouble of opening a number of fans, none of which may please her.

In the next street she sees in the window of a shop some fans, which *are open*. One of these appears to suit her, but there is no price marked on it. She does not like to go into the shop and examine more minutely whether the subtle implement she requires has sufficient strength to withstand its ball-room trials, lest it may be too expensive for her purse.

A short distance beyond another set of *opened* fans present themselves to her notice in the window of another shop, each of them with its price distinctly marked upon it. One of these the hesitating lady prefers, *a little*, to the last she had approved, and she resolves to enter this shop and examine the fan. But perceiving before she enters, that there is no attendant in the shop, she thinks the mistress may be at dinner, or have gone up stairs to her baby, and she says to herself, " It is of no consequence; I will not disturb her now."

Still passing onward she finds a shop in the window of which is a pretty fan, although not quite so good as the last, and within there sits the shop-keeper—but the door is *shut*.

Although the fan was not the most suitable the lady had seen, yet had that door been open, she would have entered, hoping that the fans exposed in the window were samples of classes kept in store within.

At last she finds all these impediments removed; a fan that will nearly suit her lies open in the window, with its price clearly marked, an attendant is in the shop, and the door is hospitably *open*. She enters and examines it, and finding it well made, asks whether there are others of the same class of pattern, to which the reply is that it is the only one remaining. Upon this she purchases the fan, although had she entered several of the former shops, she might have found fans both more exactly suited to her taste and at a less price. The *marking* has decided her choice. It is not to be imagined that all, or even the greater part of these impediments, ever occurred to one person at the same time: but there are few who have not at different times felt the effects of most of them.

§ It is said that *ladies by education and birth* occasionally amuse themselves by entering shops and giving interminable trouble, having no intention of making any purchase. This doubtlessly is a libel.

§ Several other minor impediments deter purchasers from some shops, and incline them to frequent others; amongst these may be mentioned an over officiousness in the attendants to recommend to the attention of the purchaser other articles than those he requires. This pressure to induce purchases is peculiarly offensive, and drives away the best customers.

The absence of a marked price upon an article, tends to defeat the effect of competition, as well as to produce loss of time both to consumer and vendor. It is therefore, to a certain extent, a cause of increase of price.

Its effect is to cause the same article to be sold at different prices in the same neighbourhood, thus counteracting that uniformity of price at considerable distances, which is consequent upon rapid and cheap communication.

§ As the extent to which this is carried even in a great city, may not be known, the following occurrence will afford an illustration :—

A gentleman wishing to make the light of his

reading lamp approach more nearly to day-light, looked out for a lamp-glass of a blue tint. Having observed one of the wished-for colour in a shop window marked at 1*s.* 6*d.* he purchased it. After a considerable trial he was so satisfied with the comfort it afforded to his eyes, that he wished to have other lamps in his house similarly furnished. On returning to the shop at which the blue globe was purchased, he found that its proprietor had retired, and his successor was in a different line of business. Seeing in the window of another shop in his own neighbourhood, a coloured globe of the same size, he entered and inquired the price. To his great surprise the price was stated to be 3*s.*; and on asking if any reduction would be made if he took a dozen or two, the answer was that in that case the lowest price would be half-a-crown each.

This naturally led him to suppose that the cheapness of the first glass arose from the accident of its proprietor being about to retire from business, and he therefore decided upon confining his indulgence in the luxury of white light to his single reading lamp. One day, however, he accidentally saw in another shop window a similar globe of blue glass. On inquiring within, he was informed that its price was 1*s.*, and that the price per dozen was 11*s.*

Under these new circumstances he provided a blue globe for every lamp in his house.

Now it is necessary to observe that these glasses,

charged at 3s., 1s. 6d., and 1s., were offered for
sale at three different shops not distant from each
other a mile and a half, and were not only of the
same size, weight, shade of colour and quality of
glass, but had each the same maker's stamp upon
them, and may possibly have been taken from the
same pot of glass. It is remarkable also that the
cheapest glass globe, although exposed in the shop
window, had no price attached to it.

§ It is obvious, if it were the custom invariably
to mark the price upon each article exposed for sale,
that such unreasonable differences of price in the
same article could not exist. It is certain that, if the
Royal Commissioners were to consult the dealer
who charged 3s. for an article sold by his neighbour
at 1s., they would be informed that it would
be absolutely ruinous to have prices affixed to
articles exhibited. Such a tradesman would assure
them, and with perfect truth, that it would entirely
destroy his trade. But if he cannot live upon the
ordinary profits of capital employed in his trade,
are the unwary public to pay two hundred per
cent. beyond the market price, in order to support
a tradesman unfit for his business? If, on the
other hand, the Commissioners were to ask the
opinion of the tradesman who sold the glass at 1s.,
he undoubtedly would not object to the general
practice of affixing prices to each article. The
opinion of the vendor of the glass at 1s. 6d. was

sufficiently expressed by its being attached to that article.

§ There are several causes assigned for the admitted repugnance of shopkeepers to allow the price of any article they sell to be marked upon it.

It is broadly asserted that the public, being unable to judge of the article, will be guided too much by the cheapness of its money price, neglecting its other qualities, and will thus be induced to purchase worthless things.

It is always somewhat suspicious when the vendor volunteers to take care of the interest of the purchaser. It reverses the decision of the common sense of mankind, expressed in the ancient proverb, " *caveat emptor.*" Besides, it is by no means true that the public are so ignorant or incapable of appreciating all those other qualities. In some articles the difficulty is undoubtedly great, whilst in others it may require time to be spent in their examination even by those who are as conversant with the articles as the vendor himself. But why should the time of both parties be wasted by an examination, when the price may be such as to preclude its purchase, whatever may be its other merits ?

§ Of all the various qualities which contribute to the excellence of any given article, that which it is most easy to ascertain—that which it is impossible to falsify—and that without the exact knowledge of which no purchase can possibly be made, is the very one which it is wished to withhold from the knowledge of the purchaser, until through the art of the vendor, the finer feelings of the customer induce him to think himself in some measure committed to purchase that of which he does not entirely approve.

It is from circumstances like these, that the prejudice against retail dealers arises and is confirmed in the public mind. There is no reason why that class should not be as highly respected as the possessors of extensive domains. To deserve that respect they have only to insist upon all persons in their employment abstaining from the slightest deception in serving their customers; to which rule it would be desirable to add, that the leading members of each trade should unite in discountenancing those who are guilty of any such practices.

§ The effect upon the sale of an article by the absence of its price may be illustrated by another example. Some years ago a large bazaar was held for some charitable object at the Hanover Square Rooms. It was patronised by the highest rank, and the beauty of the fair shopkeepers was even more attractive than the wares they had to dispose of. A collector thought this a favourable opportunity of adding to his collection a vase of porphyry : having paid the admission fee of 5s., he entered, and soon perceived some beautiful specimens of the object he desired. Having looked at them for some time, he selected in his mind one which he would willingly have purchased if it were within the limit (10*l*.) which he had assigned for the gratification of his taste. There was, however, no price attached to any of the vases, and fearing that they were all beyond his means, he reluctantly departed without the wished-for acquisition. It happened that he mentioned in the course of the next year the circumstance to a friend who was acquainted with the history of the vase in question. The vase for which he would willingly have given 10*l*. was not sold at that bazaar, but some time after it appeared at a less fashionable bazaar and was sold for 5*l*.

§ Most of those who visit the Exposition will each according to their means wish to retain some memorial of it. Many will have been economising during the previous year in order to purchase some object of utility or of pleasure either for their own use or to take back as remembrances to their family and friends. It would be very difficult amidst the vast variety of attractions, even if the price of each were marked upon it, to select the most desirable article within those limits of expense to which each purchaser is confined. But by forbidding the marking of prices, this difficulty is converted into an impossibility. The first step according to the decree of the Commissioners, would be to go round and ask the price of at least a hundred, if not

a thousand articles.   These must be written down
by each inquirer unless the Exhibitors supply him
with printed lists.   Even if he make a selection out of
these, it is a hundred to one that some other article
in the enormous collection would, if he had known
its price, have pleased him better.

§ If we examine the history of the earlier stages
of society, we shall see the constant tendency of its
institutions to facilitate the mutual exchange of
commodities between its members, and to remove
every obstacle impeding their interchange.   When
the population was thinly scattered over the country, the possessor of a fowl, wanting a pound of
butter, was obliged to go some distance to a neighbour either to purchase the butter or to get it
in exchange for the fowl.   But it would have cost
him more time than the worth of the butter if he
had visited several neighbours to find out where
it was the cheapest.   To remedy this inconvenience,
market days were established in the villages and
towns at more or less frequent intervals.   On
these occasions each farmer sent one of the family
to the periodic market, who sold the produce of the
farm and purchased whatever might be required of
their neighbours, who were each represented by
one of their own family at that common market.
Itinerant vendors of various manufactured articles
flocked to these markets because they there met their
customers with less loss of time and less fatigue.

Whilst these hawkers thus gained on the one hand, it must be admitted that they lost on the other those occasionally extravagant profits sometimes levied on the necessities of their isolated customers. But on the whole they derived from their trade a more regular rate of profit, because the competition side by side of rival goods and rival prices, rendered that profit much less fluctuating. Their greatest gain, however, arose from the time saved by all parties, which largely increased the consumption of their respective articles of produce.

§ When towns became enlarged, the same principle of mutual interest led to the selection of particular streets or quarters of the town by particular trades. In many cities on the continent, the jewellers, as well as some other trades, still occupy entire streets by themselves.

The next step seems to have been to hold a general exchange in a fixed spot at certain periodic times. This was necessary for the merchants and larger dealers, and for international exchanges. In great cities this was again subdivided into various branches of business, as—The Corn Exchange—The Coal Exchange, &c.

§ At these marts a class of men called brokers arose, whose business it was to sell on commission for the producers, and to purchase on commission for the merchants or other middle men.

The economy of time produced by this arrange-

ment is very great. Let us suppose an exchange
or bazaar attended by a hundred purchasers and
a hundred sellers. Each purchaser, in order to
become fully acquainted with the state of the
market, must ask at least two questions of each
seller—

    1st. What is the price?

    2d. What quantity have you for sale at that
        price?

This alone gives rise to *twenty thousand questions*.
If, on the other hand, a broker is employed, each
of the two hundred persons who constitute the
market, will have to answer those two questions
only to his own broker; consequently, there will
only be four hundred such questions. If there are
twenty brokers, these may meet together at the
market, and each stating his commissions both for
purchase and for sale, a list may be immediately
formed by which the state of the market as to supply
and demand becomes known, and in the event of
there being but little difference in the quality of the
articles, it becomes easy for the brokers to arrange
the requisite exchanges at prices which are equitable
for all parties.

   § Great, however, as this advantage is, it is small
compared with another which we shall now consider.
When a bargain is made directly by the two individuals interested in it, there usually occurs on both
sides an attempt to appear more or less indifferent

about it, in order to secure advantageous terms. Thus price is made to depend partly upon the personal feelings and qualities of the parties, and the less impulsive and more sagacious will gain considerable advantage over the hasty and inexperienced. A certain degree also of misrepresentation often occurs, and the price demanded is frequently greater than that which the seller is willing to take: thus the quantity of time consumed by parties themselves in bargaining, is always much greater than that in which their brokers can do the business for them on more advantageous terms.

Again: the broker has an interest in effecting sales, because he is paid in proportion to their amount. But he has no interest in favouring one class of his customers more than another: his profits depend entirely upon his knowledge, his industry, and his integrity. The necessity of the intervening broker arises from the imperfections of mankind, and when rigidly honest his services are invaluable. If one party is perfectly aware of all circumstances relating to the state of the market, he has no need of any broker, because he can acquire no new information: on the other hand, those who treat with him may as well save themselves the expense of a broker, because nothing can be communicated on the subject which is not already known.

When these principles, which are found to prevail in large transactions, are applied to the retail concerns of everyday life, the intervention of the broker is not required. This arises from the multitude of the transactions, the smallness of the individual amount of each, and the immense variety of the articles of exchange.

§ Another class of middle-men now come into existence, namely, Shopkeepers. The evils already pointed out still exist. One of the questions, it is true, need not be asked, for the quantity of an article held by a retail dealer, is usually much larger than the wants of any individual customer; but the question of price still remains. The removal of all these difficulties may be accomplished by the adoption of one simple plan—let the price be affixed to each article.

Other advantages result from the publicity thus given to price. Many who would not otherwise inquire the price, thinking it might be above their means, will now become purchasers. Others, not themselves intending to purchase, may incidentally cause their friends to purchase by quoting the prices they have seen affixed to certain articles. Others again, may be induced by the cheapness of an article to purchase it for uses for which it was not originally intended,—as, for instance, a beautiful chintz for papering a room.

§ In almost all works of industry, whatever may be the kind of excellence of an article exhibited, it is possible to produce one of greater excellence.

Take for instance a sheet of window-glass; its size might be adduced as the ground of excellence. The beautiful process of "*flashing*" by which it is made, is preceded by another in which the workman blows a large globe of glass. The size of the expanded flat circle of glass, called a "*table*," depends on the magnitude of this sphere, which again is limited by the power of the workman's lungs. But when larger tables were wanted, an observant workman found that if his mouth had been previously washed out with water, a greater sphere was produced. In fact, a small portion of the water, carried over with his breath, became converted into steam by the heat, and thus increased the pressure within. This led to a new limit, and there can be no doubt that by means of expensive mechanical contrivances, still larger spheres might be blown.

§ Now the whole merit of any such new process, in the eye of the manufacturer, would depend on the *price* at which the produce could be sold.

The same principle prevails in almost all works of the civil engineer. With the talent now existing in that profession, scarcely any undertaking is impossible. The real and most important limitation is the *price* of execution.

§ In the fine arts also the ultimate object still is the acquisition by the public of the productions submitted to their examination. If, however, the price is not stated, it may happen that a person of moderate means, more capable of appreciating a work of art than richer men, might be prevented from acquiring it by a feeling of delicacy. For not liking to ask the price, and thinking probably that it is beyond his means, the object may be sold to a richer competitor at a lower price than he would himself willingly have given.

This consequence of the absence of price is injurious both to art and to artists: it occasionally removes from the field of competition the best judges of real merit. It is true that in several professions a certain delicacy respecting money matters exists which is wanting in others. Medical men and artists are peculiarly subject to its influence; but it is not reported of any lawyer that he ever refused a fee, and it is recorded of some Secretary of the Admiralty that he claimed *a quarter of a year's war salary*, on account of the two days interruption of peace by the combat of Algiers.

§ Another result of the prices not being marked upon objects is, that the public are unable to form any just estimate of their commercial value; consequently, no proper public opinion arises to assist the juries in their decisions. This is a matter of considerable importance: the duty of a juror at an exposition is quite different from that of a juror in a legal question. It is the business of the Industrial juror to avail himself of the knowledge and the observations of all around him. Much of what he thus hears he may be able himself to verify by examination or experiment, and thus public opinion will be more matured, and the decisions of the juries have greater weight.

§ Many of the qualities of the articles exhibited can only be ascertained by use, or even by their destruction. In such cases a single sample would often be purchased if it had its price affixed to it.

Another class, small indeed in number, but important from its functions, suffers the greatest inconvenience from the absence of price. Those engaged in studying the commercial and economical relations of various manufactures, either for the gratification of their own tastes or for the instruction of the public, are entirely deprived of the most important element of their reasonings.

If *every article* had its price affixed, many relations would strike the eye of an experienced observer which might lead him to further inquiries, and probably to the most interesting results. But it is quite impossible for him to write to any considerable portion of 15,000 expositors for their list of prices, or even to go round and ask for it in the building itself.

§ Price in many cases offers at once a verification of the truth of other statements. Thus, to a person conversant with the subjects,

The low *price* of an article might prove that it had been manufactured in some mode entirely different from that usually practised. This would lead to an examination of it, in order to discover the improved process.

The *price* of an article compared with its weight, might prove that the metal of which it is made *could not* be genuine.

The *price* of a woven fabric, added to a knowledge of its breadth and substance, even without its weight, might in many cases effectually disprove the statement of its being entirely made of wool, or hair, or flax, or silk, as the case might be.

The exchange of commodities between those to whom such exchanges may be desirable, being the great and ultimate object of the Exposition, every circumstance that can give publicity to the things exhibited, should be most carefully attended to. The price in money is the *most important element* in every bargain ; to omit it, is not less absurd than to represent a tragedy without its hero, or to paint a portrait without a nose.

It commits a double error : for it withholds the only test by which the comparative value of things can be known, and it puts aside the greatest of all interests, that of the consumer, in order to favour a small and particular class—the middle-men.

The composition of that Commission must be most extraordinary, where an error so contrary to

the principles and so fatal to the objects of the
Exposition, could have been committed. It is not
too late to apply at least a partial remedy to the
evil, and it is scarcely credible that those with
whom it rests, can remain unconscious of the mistake into which they have been led.

§ At the eighth meeting of the Commissioners,
on the 28th Feb. 1850, further conditions and
limitations were submitted to them by Col. Reid,
one of which was—

"A price may be attached to the objects exhibited, and
the objects, if sold, may be marked; but no sales will be
permitted within the building."

This judicious recommendation was, however,
not adopted, for on the 11th April, 1850, the following rule was published—

"The Exhibition being intended for the purposes of display
only, and not for those of sale. . . .
"For the same reason the Commissioners have decided that
the prices are not to be affixed to the articles exhibited."

Several strong remonstrances were addressed to
the Commissioners against the rule forbidding the
affixing prices to the articles exhibited. Efforts
were made both in public and through private
representations to some of its individual members,
by persons competent to advise, and anxious for
the success of a great and meritorious undertaking.

In the report of the Leeds Committee to the Commissioners the following passage occurs :—

" They are, further, most strongly of opinion that the statement of price is essential, *if the Exhibition is to be of any real utility.* To the manufacturer or merchant price will be the test of comparative value and excellence in the majority of cases ; and the inspection of particular fabrics, especially the products of other districts or countries, for the purposes of information or improvement, will be of no avail to them if price as well as style and finish is not before them."

From the secretary to the Hamburg Commission a communication was received stating that—

" In consequence of the decision of the Commissioners with respect to the prohibition to attach prices, it is the opinion that there will be an *incurable deficiency* in the Exhibition."

From the Central Danish Commission a letter was sent, stating that—

" By reason of the regulation of Her Majesty's Commissioners that prices may not be attached to articles sent for exhibition, and Danish goods being chiefly remarkable for their cheapness, a space of about 450 square ft. will be sufficient for Denmark."

The Chevalier Bunsen transmitted a despatch from the Prussian government, *objecting to the decision* of the Commissioners which *prohibits the affixing of prices* to articles exhibited.

§ On the 14th November, 1850, an answer to this letter was approved, and ordered to be sent to all foreign commissioners.

The following are extracts :—

" The arguments advanced by you in favour of authorizing the affixing of prices to the articles exhibited, have received the maturest consideration of Her Majesty's Commissioners, who are fully sensible of the great importance of the subject.

" At the same time, every wish is felt on their part, to give to each exhibitor the *benefit* to be derived by him from the knowledge on the part of the public, of the cheapness of the articles exhibited by him. They feel, however, as they have already intimated, that by allowing the affixing of the actual prices to articles themselves, they should be making themselves responsible for the accuracy of those prices in all instances, and they would not consider themselves warranted in assuming this responsibility in the case of an Exhibition of the productions of all the nations in the world (however perfect may be the machinery in an individual country, like Prussia, for ensuring that accuracy, and for preventing the liability to deception). But Her Majesty's Commissioners authorize the attachment of a notice to those Goods, of which the merit consists in the low price at which they can be produced, to the effect that they are *exhibited for cheapness*, and they have made it a condition that all persons making this claim must send the prices in an invoice to the Commissioners, who will instruct the juries to make this an essential element in their determination of their awards."

The Decision No. 16 was then altered as follows :—

" Prices are not to be affixed to the articles exhibited, although the articles may be marked as shown for economy of production. But as the cost at which articles can be produced will, in some cases, enter into the question of the distribution of rewards, the Commissioners, or the persons intrusted with the adjudication of the rewards, may have to make inquiries, and possibly to take evidence, upon the subject ; still they do not consider it expedient to affix a note of

the price to the articles displayed. When the Exhibitor
considers the merit of his article to consist in its cheapness,
and founds a claim on this ground, he must state the price in
the invoice sent to the Commissioners."

This rule is a model specimen of what very clever
men united in a large committee can assent to.

The first and last sentences of the oracular
writing pronounce that—

Prices must not be affixed to any article exhibited for the judgment of the public, *even though*
there should be *no other reason* for exhibiting it
than its price.

The intervening sentence reveals to us that even
Commissioners may in some cases be themselves
unable to judge without a knowledge of the price—
that it may perchance be so important that they
must take evidence upon it. Yet, with a very
flattering deference to the sagacity of the public,
they seem to think *it* can, without that information,
form as good an opinion as their own.

It may be remarked that the permission to ask
of the attendant the price of an article, on which
much stress has been laid, depends on several contingencies, namely :—that every article has an attendant ;—that he is at all times at his post ;—and
also that he *knows* its price.

It is admitted that the Commissioners wish " to
" give each exhibitor the *benefit* to be derived by
" him from the knowledge [of price] on the part of
" the public," and also that the public cannot judge

without that information, and yet, with singular inconsistency, they forbid the simplest and most natural mode of accomplishing this object, placing in fact an impediment in the way of their own wishes.

The only argument which is urged in favour of this rule, occurs in the reply to the Prussian application, in which it is stated, "after the maturest " consideration on the part of Her Majesty's Com- " missioners," they feel "that by allowing the affix- " ing the actual price to the articles themselves, " they should be making themselves responsible for " the accuracy of those prices in all instances." This singular timidity in fact involves the Commissioners in far larger responsibility, since according to their own argument they admit that they are " *responsible*" for any statement they " *allow*" the exhibitors to make ; it follows, therefore, that any statement they *command* the exhibitors to attach to the articles exposed must be still more firmly *guaranteed* by the Commissioners.

But they have very rightly ordered that every article shall have attached to it a statement of the *reason* for which it is exhibited. Consequently *they guarantee the statements made by exhibitors.*

If, therefore, a piece of calico is exhibited entirely for the sake of the *permanence* of the beautiful colour with which it is dyed, the beauty it is true may be evident to the eye, but the merit will consist wholly in the *permanence*. If this is stated by the exhibitor, the Commissioners themselves are responsible for its truth.

Again, some beautiful damasked fabric is exhibited ; the only merit consists in its being made entirely of flax. This statement must be appended, or there is no use in exhibiting it ; but if stated, the *Commissioners are responsible* that there is no silk intermixed : multitudes of similar cases might be adduced.

But the truth is, that no such responsibility as that which they have assumed, ought to be placed on the Commissioners ; their duty is sufficiently arduous, and their previous experience very limited. A certain per centage of error and accident, will necessarily occur, even to the most highly informed, and if they industriously exercise the knowledge they may acquire in carrying on this undertaking, the public ought to be grateful for their labours— to assist them in carrying out their regulations, and remonstrate strongly only when their rules violate the very foundations of those principles on which the whole advantage of the Exposition rests.

§ Nothing could have been more simple than to have repudiated any such guarantee, and to have left the public to trust to the integrity and honour of the exhibitors, which, considering the danger and facility of detection, would have been a sufficient security. The Royal, and almost all other scientific

Societies, place at the head of each volume a distinct declaration that their authors alone are responsible, both for the facts as well as for the reasonings contained in their respective memoirs.

§ If the alternative were proposed, Shall the rule rigidly laid down be ?—

" No article shall have its price marked on " it" — or,

" Every article must have its price marked upon " it,"—the disadvantages would be far less under the latter rule. The essential principle of the Exposition being the increase of commerce and the exchange of commodities, it might even be contended that sales should be permitted on the premises. The chief objection to this arises from the impediments it might offer to the free access of visitors to the examination of the articles exhibited.

Means, however, might be suggested by which that objection would be considerably removed. It might, for instance, be permitted to all those exhibitors of articles of moderate size, that they should bring in with them each morning a sufficient number of such articles, done up in paper ready to be delivered to the purchaser on his handing over the money price. This would apply to a large number of articles, as shawls, dresses, &c.

In other articles, sold by weight, packets might be previously made up of various weights, as one pound, three pounds, six pounds, &c. In those sold by length, parcels of fixed numbers of yards might be prepared.

If this system were still thought to be inconvenient from causing crowds in particular spots, it might be permitted to the attendants to take orders for articles to be sent home in the evening, and paid for either at the time or on delivery.

It is quite certain that under either of these conditions a much larger quantity of merchandize would be sold immediately.

Many would purchase on the spot who could never return for that purpose, or who were on the point of leaving London, and much trouble would be saved to a large class of purchasers.

The effect of the purchases made in the earlier days of the Exposition, would act as so many advertisements to attract visitors on the succeeding days; some articles thus purchased would probably be sent into the country by friends, and others be taken home by visitors, and many additional country visitors would thus be attracted before the end of the season.

Another and a very important advantage would also accrue from such an arrangement. The manufacturers acquire their knowledge of the demand for their productions from the factors and agents; these again from the shopkeepers who sell by retail to the public. Under the proposed circumstances, this knowledge would be acquired much more rapidly, and in the course of the first two or three weeks the opinion of the public would be known upon all the articles of most popular demand.

§ Upon the whole, the best plan seems to be that the rule should be—

" Every article must have its price attached."

The exception should be exemptions granted by officers of the Commission, and the ground of those exemptions should be stated on the respective articles.

At the Exposition at Paris, in 1849, the general rule was that upon each article its price should be marked. Certain exceptions occurred, and in two instances the writer of these pages wishing to purchase specimens, although assisted most willingly by M. Le Dieu, the indefatigable head of the management always present on the spot, was unable, after some correspondence and much inquiry, to purchase or obtain samples of the objects he desired.

§ Perhaps the best way of complying with the rules of the Commissioners, and yet giving the public what they tacitly admit the public will demand, would be that the exhibitor should fix on each of his articles, in a conspicuous manner, a letter or a number,* and that he should have on the

---

* As by one of the rules each separate article exhibited must have a number, the same numbers might be used in the bills.

printed bill or card of address all the corresponding numbers or letters, and opposite to each the price at which it was to be sold at his warehouse or place of business. Each expositor might have a quantity of these addresses hung up or placed upon his stall, with an indication to the public that they were at liberty to take away these cards or bills.

It may be worth while to make a few observations on the reasons which probably influenced and misled the Commission on so important a point.

The tradesmen of London had been unduly and rather indelicately pressed to subscribe towards the Exposition; many were compelled to subscribe against their wishes. They saw few or none of the advantages which would accrue to them from it, and they believed, (erroneously,) that it would inundate the country with foreign and cheaper articles that would supplant their own trade.

It was thought that, when the public became acquainted with the wholesale as well as with the retail price of articles, such knowledge would lead to a reduction of the retail profits. The public, it was argued, would be reluctant to make a fair allowance for the various items which contribute to swell the amount of the difference between the wholesale and retail price of commodities.

§ It may be useful then to state broadly the principle, that it is greatly for the advantage of the public, both as regards economy of time and of money, that there should always exist a sufficient number of middle-men of various orders.

The shopkeeper, who is the one in immediate contact with the public, and therefore liable to the greatest misrepresentation, has, amongst others, the following expenses to add to the cost of production, which must necessarily increase the retail price :—

1. Commission to broker or other middle-man.

2. Cost of carriage from manufactory to shop.

3. Rent of shop itself, and perhaps, also of a warehouse.

4. Insurance of stock against fire.

5. Attendants to sell in shop.

6. Sending goods home to purchasers.

7. Expense of paper, string, &c. for packing goods delivered.

8. Loss by plunder of servants.

9. Expense of taking stock to diminish this loss.

10. Goods soiled or injured by exposing to sale.

11. Goods going out of fashion, cheapened by improved manufacture, or superseded by new inventions.

12. Giving long credit.

13. Bad debts.

14. Payment for his own personal services, as retail trader.

15. Interest on capital employed.

§ Admitting, however, that these grounds fully

account for a large difference between the wholesale and retail price, they will by no means justify several practices which are too frequent at some shops at the west end of the town.

Different prices for the very same article are often demanded by retail tradesmen, according to the supposed position of the purchaser. Fish, for example, which varies much in price, and is at times very cheap, will seldom be found charged in the household bill much below the average price, unless the housekeeper is honest and looks sharply after the matter. Few circumstances more annoy a customer or are more injurious to the tradesman than this offence of having two prices.

When the same prices are charged equally to all customers, it often happens that it is much higher in the western than in less fashionable localities. This may arise from a vicious system of giving credit, and the extra price is necessary to compensate for risk of loss, and of capital lying unproductive. The effect, however, is injurious to the tradesman: many of those who pay ready money and would therefore be his best customers, desert the shop. Those whose means are small, go to a greater distance for the daily or weekly purchases; whilst those possessed of larger incomes, purchase the same articles, not only at a cheaper shop in the city but in larger quantities, and therefore more nearly at the wholesale price.

Our foreign visitors naturally ask how it happened that in the country of Adam Smith so
strange a mistake could have been made : they
inquire why none of the eminent disciples of that
school were placed on the Commission ? They will
learn with surprise that our Minister of Commerce
took, as befitted his office, an active part in it;
that the great economist, to whose profound views
and extensive experience in monetary affairs more
than one minister has been indebted, was also a
member; that even the apostle of *free trade* himself, whose successful exertions have been crowned
with merited reward, sat on the same commission ;
and yet that the talents, the knowledge, and the
eloquence of such men, failed to convince the understandings of their colleagues, who, in violation
of the first principles of " *Free trade*," deliberately
raised an obstacle against *competition*.

Since the first edition of this work was printed,
the Crystal Palace has been filled by the industry
and peopled by the nations of the earth.   The
fears of the ignorant, the hopes of the selfish, the
vaticinations of the shallow, have proved alike
groundless.   Opinions expressed by the few who
were competent to judge, which were then scouted
as the ravings of visionaries, have now become
realized as facts.

However great the admitted advantages resulting from the Exposition have been, still it has failed

to produce anything like the information which it was calculated to afford. Many of those who most rejoice in its success regret that so much perseverance and energy have not, owing to one fatal error, been permitted to accomplish the full amount of good which they so well deserved to have achieved.

The public have now had ample opportunity of forming their own opinion upon the question of *price;* and they are almost unanimous in their decision that without having the *price* on the articles they examine, the collection is of little intrinsic use to them, although it is a very agreeable and splendid show.

No attempt to answer the arguments on that question contained in the first edition of this work has yet reached me. An entirely different reason has now been assigned for the omission of *price.*

It is asserted that the shopkeepers of London persuaded the Commissioners that if *prices* were permitted to be fixed upon articles, they, the shopkeepers, would destroy the Exhibition, by not exhibiting anything themselves, and by their determination ruin the producer, if, by affixing prices to his produce, he should expose the "*secrets of trade.*"

One of the proverbs most frequently appealed to is — deprecation of *protection* by one's *friends:* few cases have ever occurred in which its application is more necessary.

These friends thus maintain that the reason for *forbidding prices* to be placed upon articles, stated by the Commissioners to have been arrived at after mature consideration, and *officially* communicated by them to foreign governments,—was not the *real reason*.

The motive of the rule laid down by the Commission seems to have been a conscientious wish not to mislead the public, and was at most only an error of judgment.

The *friends* of the Commission, however, have imputed to them a line of conduct which, to use the mildest form of expression, is highly undignified, and have suggested that they were driven to the adoption of the rule by fears which were absurd.

Some of the fashionable shopkeepers at the West-end may have endeavoured to alarm their too credulous customers by holding out such exaggerated estimates of their own power ; but the mass of London tradesmen are a shrewder race, and estimate more truly their own influence. They well know, in the present state of rapid communication throughout the land, that any such attempt must necessarily fail. Imagine for a moment the present race of butchers attempting to starve London by combining to withhold meat. The utmost they could accomplish, if so inclined, would be to put their customers to some small and temporary inconvenience, at the expense of certain ruin to themselves.

The practical effect of forbidding prices has been very unfortunate. The great and meritorious efforts by which the plan has been carried out, have been shorn of much of their utility. A building of half the size, containing only articles *each* of which had attached to it a short and clear statement of the grounds on which it was exhibited, and the price at which it could be acquired, would have conveyed far more instruction to the public, and have been far more effective for the promotion of commerce, thus fulfilling much more completely the two great objects of the Exposition.

To reply that prices may be obtained on inquiry, betrays a childish ignorance of the whole subject. It is practically impossible to obtain the required information; and those who have made the effort, have found that even in the cases where an attendant is present to explain the articles, he is often entirely ignorant of their price.

The effect of the absence of price on visitors is a source of painful annoyance to themselves, and of loss to the manufacturers and shopkeepers, from whom they would otherwise have purchased largely.

Foreigners are so sensible of this defect, that they have in many instances printed priced catalogues of their own articles. Their interpretation of our refusal to allow prices to be affixed is, that we are unable to compete with other nations in economy of production.

H

The philosopher and the economist, by whose researches and comparisons the public might have been instructed, wander through the lofty avenues and splendid galleries of the Crystal Palace, tantalized by expectations, raised but to be disappointed. They at last are compelled to abandon their mission in hopeless despair, wilfully deprived, by the managers of this industrial feast, of that information on which all their conclusions must ultimately rest.

CHAPTER IX.

THE great feature of the original plan of the Exposition was to give large prizes. One, at least, was to have been 5,000*l.*, and the whole amount of them 20,000*l.*

The anticipation of these prizes gave hope and industry to thousands: means were examined and measures taken by many a workman, at the expense of great personal sacrifices, to enable him to complete a model of some favourite scheme, by which he might hope to win one amongst the many pecuniary prizes, and thus be repaid at least for a portion of his efforts.

The announcement on the Continent of these liberal arrangements was received with unbounded astonishment and admiration. The magnitude of the great prize seemed to foreigners incredible, and the liberality of offering it to the competing world, was altogether beyond their conception of the character assigned to us as a nation.

It was certainly very unfortunate that such an

announcement should have been made and then withdrawn. But as the question will probably arise again, it may be useful for some future occasion to inquire now into the principles on which pecuniary prizes should be awarded.

Science, literature, and industrial art are in some measure subject to the same laws in the distribution of pecuniary rewards. It is desirable that such prizes should be given to those objects only which, possessing very considerable merit and utility, are of such a nature as not to repay the first inventors.

§ One effect of such rewards would be to increase very much the number of minds engaged in making inventions. This itself is a matter of more importance than might at first be thought as will be shown on some future occasion in examining the question of monopoly.

The inventor, the capitalist, and the manufacturer of articles are usually distinct persons. Of these the inventor is generally the least rewarded. The capitalist and the manufacturer can almost always make their own way to wealth, and if successful their reward is usually large, and almost always greater even than the highest prize which could be offered by the managers of such an Exhibition as is now contemplated.

If it were a condition for obtaining a prize that no patent should be taken out, then the prize may

be considered as the purchase money of the patent
for the use of the public. If a patent is desired by
the inventor, a medal or an honorary prize might
be given, with the addition in certain cases of a
reward in money.

Perhaps an enumeration of some objects which
might become fit subjects for prizes, may best illustrate these views.

§ One of the inventions most important to a class
of highly skilled workmen (engineers) would be
a small motive power,—ranging perhaps from the
force of half a man, to that of two horses, which might
commence as well as cease its action at a moment's
notice, require no expense of time for its management, and be of moderate price both in original
cost and in daily expense. A small steam-engine
does not fulfil these conditions. In a town where
water is supplied at high-pressure, a cylinder and a
portion of apparatus similar to that of a high-pressure engine, would fully answer the conditions, if
the water could be supplied at a moderate price.
Such a source of power would in many cases be invaluable to men just rising from the class of jour-
neyman to that of master. It might also be of
great use to many small masters in various trades.
If the cost per day were even somewhat greater
than that of steam for an equal extent of power,
it would yet be on the whole much cheaper,
because it would *never consume power without doing*

work. It might be applied to small planing and drilling machines, to lathes, to grindstones, grinding mills, mangling, and to a great variety of other purposes.

§ In all large workshops a separate tool, or rather machine, is used for each process, and this contributes to the economy of the produce. But many masters in a small way are unable to afford such an expense, not having sufficient work for the full employment of any one machine.

Of this class are many jobbing masters who live by repairing machines. Such also are that class of masters who make models of the inventions of others and carry out for them their mechanical speculations. To these two classes, that of amateur engineers may be added.

The lathe with its sliding rest is the basis of their stock. With this they can drill, and with the addition of a few wheels can cut screws. The further addition of a vertical slide will enable them to plane small pieces of metal by means of facing cutters on the mandril. By other additions the teeth of wheels may also be cut, and in some rare cases, a lathe may be converted into a small planing machine. The loss of time in making the changes necessary to enable the lathe to fulfil all these different functions, necessarily confines its use to the peculiar classes alluded to above, but to make these changes is often less expensive than to be obliged continually to send to larger workshops where the heavier portion of their work can be executed. It would certainly be desirable, if some good plan cannot be devised for bringing the whole of such operations within the reach of *one* machine of moderate price, that at least a system should be devised for combining them in *two* separate machines.

Some readers may possibly think such combinations as have been mentioned, too minute and special for the ubject of a prize: but when it is considered that they bear upon the interests of one of the best classes of workmen, and how important it is for the welfare of the community that skill, industry, and intelligence should be assisted in their efforts to rise in the social scale, these details will be excused.

§ The improvements which have been made in the economy of working voltaic batteries, lead to the expectation that they may be employed as sources of artificial light. Although the light thus obtained is not yet sufficiently steady for general use, it may possibly become available for light-houses.

Galvanic light offers some advantages for this purpose on account of its intensity and of the facility it affords for darkening and restoring the light, by breaking and renewing the galvanic circuit.

But it would be possible to adapt the same

principle of occultations to ordinary lighthouses. It would only be necessary to apply mechanism which should periodically pull down an opaque shade over the glass cylinders of the argand burners. This should be instantaneously thrown back by a spring. A series of obscurations corresponding to the digits of any number, and separated by any intervals, might thus be continually repeated.

Ready means might thus be supplied of clearly distinguishing one light-house from another. For this purpose it would be necessary to denote the light-houses on any coast by different numbers.

Any digit might be expressed by an equivalent number of occultations and restorations of the light: thus—

1	2	3	9
0.0	0.0.0	0.0.0.0, &c.,	0.0.0.0.0.0.0.0.0

Again, the character of the digit might be indicated by occultations preceded and followed, by shorter or longer intervals of light.

At the commencement, the first digit of any number, might be distinguished by a previous uniform continuance of the light during ten or twenty seconds, whilst the separation of each digit from the next in order might be denoted by a short pause of two or three or more seconds.

Thus, if the number of a light-house were 253 : after a cessation of any obscuration during ten

seconds, two occultations should follow each other
at intervals of about a second. A pause should
then occur during three seconds, after which five
occultations should occur, at intervals of one
second, as before. Another pause of three seconds
must then happen, and be succeeded by three
other occultations occurring at intervals of one
second each; after which ten seconds must elapse
before the cycle thus described is repeated.

These might be thus represented :—

2 hundreds.   5 tens.   3 units.

0000000000·0·000·0·0·0·0·000·0·0·0000000000

Thus, at about every half minute the number
of the lighthouse would be repeated.

In this manner any number under 1,000 may be
expressed in less than one minute; since the largest,
999, would require

	Seconds.
For each digit 9, or in all	27
Two short pauses between the digits . . .	6
One long long pause at end of the number .	10
	43

Every light-house, therefore, would be continually
repeating its own number.

It would contribute still more to prevent mistakes,
if the light-houses on a coast were not numbered
in succession; for should any mistake be made in
counting the obscurations, it would most probably

be detected if the digits of the numbers of the light-houses on the same part of the coast were as different as possible.

Lighthouse numbered in succession—

| 234 | 235 | 236 | 237 | 238 |

Ditto irregularly—

| 142 | 324 | 581 | 787 | 612 |

If a mistake of a single obscuration were made in the units of the number 237, and it had been counted 236, this observation might, until repeated, mislead the sailor, and induce him to suppose himself opposite the preceding light-house. On the contrary, if the irregular mode of numbering were adopted, the mistake of 786 for 787 could not mislead, because the seven in the hundreds place would point out the error. It would, however, be better to have the figure in the tens' place also different in any two light-houses so near that a possibility of mistake is likely to occur. The general benefit which would result to all maritime nations, renders the practical application of these principles a peculiarly fit subject for a prize.

Since the first edition of this work was published, an occulting light has been exhibited for about three weeks, representing during each night the constant repetition of one of the following numbers, 136, 227, 354, 432.

As might easily have been anticipated, its effect

was quite satisfactory in determining those numbers. At about a distance of a quarter of a mile, its occultations were even more distinct than at shorter distances.

Successive improvements have occurred, until it now seems desirable to revise and simplify the lighthouses of the world, by making them speak one universal language, intelligible even to the commonest capacity. No time could be more favourable than the present for establishing an international system of signals, founded on numbers, and adapted to the wants and convenience of all nations. The following brief outline of such a plan requires, therefore, no apology.

The present modes of identifying lighthouses are by

1. The *colour* of the lights.
2. The *number, distance,* and *relative position* of the lights exhibited.
3. The *variations* in colour or intensity, or in the time during which the lights are partially or totally obscured, compared with that during which they are visible.
4. By striking bells or gongs in foggy weather.

There are around the coasts of Great Britain about 290 light-houses and light-ships. They exhibit nearly 390 lights. Of these, about one hundred lights are coloured, chiefly red. Fifty-five are revolving lights, varying in their periods from five seconds to four minutes. In foggy weather fifteen of these toll bells, and thirty-three strike gongs. It is proposed to abolish all the revolving lights, and to retain white light, to distinguish by its occultations the number of the light-house which it is destined to indicate.

With respect to those lighthouses which indicate ports, next to the information as to the name of the port, the most important question is the depth of water at its entrance. This may be given by allowing the occultations of the white light to indicate the number of the port, after which a glass of green or of any other colour being interposed, the number of occultations mark the number of feet of the depth of water at the time.

A float in a well, to which the tide has access by a small aperture, will serve the double purpose of raising the weight that drives the mechanism for occulting, and of prescribing, according to the height of the tide in feet, the corresponding number of occultations of the green light.

Thus a constant alternation will go on during the whole night of repetitions of the *number* of the port, by occultations of white light, and of the number of feet which indicate the depth of water at its entrance, by green light.

There are certain cases of obscuration of lights

by fog in which bells and gongs are continually sounded. These convey information of danger, but do not identify its position. The same principle which gives numerical accuracy to lighthouses, and even the same mechanism, may be made to operate during fogs with equal effect on sounds. Thus, by striking the gong the requisite number of times to indicate the hundreds, the tens, and the units denoting the light, allowing, of course, the usual pauses and the same long intervals, the number of the light-house or lightship may be known as quickly and as certainly by means of bells, or gongs, or other sounds, as by the occultations of its light.

It may be worth examining what musical notes are heard at the greatest distances through fogs, and the sounds of what instruments penetrate farthest amidst the roar of winds and waves. The shrill whistle of the steam carriage should be tried against the deep tones of the organ and the loud noise of the trumpet. The most powerful sounds produced by air require but little physical force for their generation; and whenever the directions in which it is necessary to give warning are known, the sounds employed may be concentrated by reflectors, in the same manner as light.

The depth of water at the entrance of harbours may easily be indicated in the day-time by a tide-telegraph governed by the same float which produces the occultations during the night. Its form may be as below,

in which the arms projecting on the left side indicate the tens; those on the right side the units. The long arm for the fifth saves trouble in counting. These arms must be movable on centres within the mast, and must be governed by cams connected with the float, so as to indicate at any time the state of the tide. If it were found necessary to distinguish light-houses during the day, then signs expressing their permanent numbers might be painted upon them, or fixed to masts rising out of each. The right side of the telegraph might, if required, be used as a day telegraph for communicating with vessels.

By means of such light-houses it would be easy to convey telegraphic messages either to vessels in distress, or for other purposes. It would simply be required to use the light itself or a subsidiary one to indicate a series of numbers corresponding to those in some known Telegraphic Dictionary. No danger of any mistake could arise during the few minutes thus employed, because any other vessel on counting the succession of obscurations would not only perceive that the light-house was telegraphing, but would also know the object of the message. A small apparatus might easily be contrived for the use of vessels, by which they might ask any questions necessary for their safety. Such means for ships sailing in company, or even for fleets, might enable them to proceed on their voyage during the night, and to communicate any orders even with greater facility than in the day.

Sir David Brewster proposed in the *Edinburgh Philosophical Transactions* a plan for distinguishing light-houses by optical means. The light transmitted through a thin film, when analysed by a prism, appears either single, or subdivided into two, three, four or more parts. Light-houses, therefore, might thus be distinguished from one another numerically.

CHAPTER X.

A CLEAR statement of the *principles* on which each jury is to award prizes, should be placed before them. These principles ought to be well discussed, and in that discussion manufacturers should be invited to take a part.

The first object of the jury should be to lay down rules by which these principles are to be carried out. Each class of the subjects to be rewarded will have its own rules. They will generally be few in number, and capable of being expressed in few words: some of these are suggested below, but merely by way of example.

One of the most general rules will indicate the means by which the jury can ascertain the fact, that the material of the manufacture under consideration is truly the substance it is represented to be.

For instance: some woven fabric is examined, professing to be made either entirely of wool, or wholly of flax. It may be quite true that experienced manufacturers and dealers, are able to detect any adulteration of either material by admixture with the other. But statements of facts made on authority, never possess the same weight with the public as those which are accompanied by information enabling any individual among that public to verify the fact for himself.

The form of the fibre as shown by the microscope is one test. A more simple one is to burn some fibres in the flame of a candle. Every fibre which, when thus treated, produces the smell of burnt feathers, is animal matter of some kind, as wool, silk, horse-hair, &c. The burnt fibres of hemp, flax, cotton, and other vegetable matters have a totally different scent; a fact of which any one may readily assure himself by making the experiment.

It may perhaps be necessary in some cases to wash the fabric under examination, lest in what is termed the "getting up for the market," some animal matter or size might mislead. But the jury ought to be acquainted with all such difficulties, and they should state the method they took for investigating them.

The microscope is of great use in the detection of adulterations in most vegetable substances.

§ Every object produced is subject to certain defects, and possessed of certain excellences: these should be clearly enumerated. Whenever such

I

statements are expressed by numbers, the information will be more satisfactory.

Thus, in cutting tools, as applied to various metals, it is very important that the angle at which the tool is applied, should be stated : it is also necessary to state the angle which the edge of the tool receiving the shaving cut off, makes with the surface cut. The velocity of the tool in cutting should be stated, also the names of the fluids, if any, used in cutting.

The durability of woven fabrics, as well as of a great variety of other manufactured articles, is a most essential quality, on which, combined with the price, their chief value to the customer depends.

It is very desirable that the jury should find satisfactory means of testing this most important character, which is not discernible, even by the most curious and instructed spectator.

The knowledge of the weight required for tearing asunder any woven fabric, as a ribbon, a stay-lace, tape, &c., together with the breaking weight of their individual threads, and the number of these threads in an inch, may in some cases be very valuable, especially in coarse articles, such as sailcloth, sacking, &c.

In other cases, the articles may be submitted to twenty or thirty washings and dryings, during which it may repeatedly be examined. The greatest change will most frequently occur on the first washing, which removes the dressing.

§ In many articles the durability of different parts varies considerably. In some cases one part will wear out, if replaced, many times before the remainder of the article is at all injured by use. In all such cases the jury should adopt such rules as the following :—

Examine the durability of each part, and also the difficulty and the expense of replacing it when injured.

Examine also, for the same purpose, what parts are most exposed to injury or destruction by accident.

Examine also the *relative* expense of putting the article in a working state when first purchased and brought home.

These rules will be best understood by an illustration. Let us suppose a jury to be examining the relative merits of several cottage stoves for cooking. Of course the first inquiry will be as to which admits of the best performance of the operations of—

Boiling,	Baking,
Stewing,	Supply of hot water,
Roasting,	Ironing,
Broiling,	&c.

The cost of the fuel must not only be given, but also its weight, because the price of fuel varies in different localities. The capability of using different sorts of fuel in the several stoves, and the amount of fuel so consumed for its equivalent of coal, should also be stated.

These and other comparative inquiries having been made, the durability of that part of the stove which is subjected to the direct action of the burning fuel, must be examined. It will be made either of iron or of earthenware; and the relative merit of the various stoves will, as far as this point is concerned, consist in the facility and economy with which such parts can be removed, and the corresponding new parts be purchased and replaced in their proper position. It is always desirable for the consumer that the vendors of such articles should keep a stock of the parts liable to wear out, and that the latter should undertake to replace them at a fixed price.

Those parts of the stove which project so as to be liable to accidental blows, and those which from their more constant use are much exposed to accident, as the hinges and the latches of doors, should then be examined. These, if of cast-iron or other brittle material, and constituting part of the substance of the door, should be sufficiently strong to resist fracture: if they are attached to it by rivets or otherwise, they will be lighter and stronger when made of wrought-iron.

The last inquiry is into the expense of fixing the stove for use. It may be set in brickwork, within

the chimney, in which case it will require a brick-
layer and a large mass of materials in the shape of
bricks and mortar, and possibly of stone. Or it
may stand on its own base containing its own ash-pit.
and by means of a small iron pipe the smoke may
be conveyed into a flue. In this case almost any
workman with hammer and chisel and a small
quantity of mortar or cement, can fix it ready for
use.

Again, the stop-cock for the water-cistern may be
either hard-soldered, riveted, or screwed in. If the
latter, it can easily be unscrewed or reground when
necessary. The same remark applies to the leaden
supply-pipe; it may be connected by soldering, or
by a union joint. In the former case these parts
will require the aid not only of the tinman or copper-
smith, but also of the plumber.

§ The expense of repairing a machine does not in
all cases depend on the cost of the part replaced, or
even on the actual cost of replacing that part alone.
It often happened in the earlier days of loco-
motive engines, that the expense of some small
reparation necessary to keep the machine in good
working order, did not amount to ten shillings;
whilst the expense of removing and replacing other
parts, without which the workman could not get at
the defective part, amounted to fifty or eighty shillings, or even to a still larger sum.

Thus facility of getting at all the parts of an

engine for the purposes of repair, or even of examination, is one of the advantages which the broad
possesses over the narrow gauge.

§ In many articles exposed to great or sudden
force, and to much wear and tear, it is very desirable that if any breakage occur, it should happen
at that point where the consequences would be the
least dangerous to the persons using it, and the
reparation of it least expensive.

During a series of experiments made by the
author in 1839, on the Great Western Railway, it
was necessary, amongst a variety of other curves, to
cause a pen to draw upon long rolls of paper the
curve described by the centre of a carriage, pro-
jected on the plane of the road.   When everything
is in proper order, this line ought to be parallel to,
and in the middle between, the two rails.   But it is
well known that instead of answering these conditions, it often describes a *serpentine* curve, arising
from that snake-like motion of a train which the
carriages acquire by rolling alternately towards each
rail, until they are checked by the flanges pressing
against it.

To accomplish the drawing of the line above-
mentioned, it was necessary to have depending
from the carriage, a very stout jointed wooden arm,
terminating in an iron *shoe* with a steel projection.
This *shoe* was, by a powerful spring, pressed close
to the rail in the middle point between the two side

wheels of the carriage, and by a communication with the pen the required curve was described.

But such an apparatus was exposed to very rough work, and, in fact, was generally broken three or four times during each experimental journey. If the broken part had fallen between the wheel and the rail, it might have caused a serious accident. To prevent this the following precautions were taken—

The wooden arm was strengthened with thin strips of iron, except at one part about an inch long. At this part of the wood a small notch was cut with a saw. The lower portion had a strong iron eye fixed into it, which was connected loosely to a hook by a rope passing through a hole in the middle of the carriage.

Whenever the apparatus broke, it was always at the notch. The position of the loose rope holding the broken part was such, that the tendency was immediately to drag it into the middle of the road under the centre of the carriage. This at once removed it from interference with the wheels. The pen describing the curve soon gave notice by ceasing to move laterally, that the arm was broken; on which one of the assistants immediately took hold of the loose rope, and pulling the broken fragment close up to the bottom of the carriage, prevented the possibility of any further danger.

§ If each jury were to explain concisely the

means employed by them to examine the qualities of each class of objects submitted to them, much valuable information would result. A collection of these rules for the judgment or verification of articles, if reduced into order, and published in a small compass, by a competent person, at the close of the Exposition, would be invaluable to the public. The result would be beneficial to all *honest* tradesmen, and injurious only to the *fradulent*. Such means when put into the hands of the public would soon enable it to distinguish the genuine from the sophisticated articles, and to select those which in point of excellence and durability are best suited to the means or wants of the purchaser.* The increased knowledge of the public would be felt by the retail dealers, and would make them more anxious to obtain excellent and durable goods from the manufacturer.

§ Several of the papers issued by the Commission bear honourable testimony to the sagacity of those who composed them. They treat the persons addressed as reasoning men, explaining to them the results contemplated : thus whilst offering their own most strenuous exertions, they admit that these would scarcely prove effective without the co-operation of the public in a plan devised for the common advantage of all.

* Several valuable papers containing rules of this kind have lately appeared in the *Lancet*.

In former days had there been water-fowl in our parks, some such notice as this would have been placarded :—

" Whoever throws stones at, or frightens these " birds, shall be prosecuted with the utmost severity " of the law."

In the present day we read the much more effective address,

" These birds are recommended to the protection " of the public."

However ragged the coat of the passer-by, his feelings not his fears are addressed, and his pride is gratified by being appointed as it were a temporary trustee for the safety of his feathered friends. The advantage of acting upon this principle is not confined merely to its direct efficiency for its purpose. A still more important benefit remains latent, one which never ought to be lost sight of in the enactment or the administration of laws.

*It enlists public opinion in favour of law and of order.**

* The ancient law of rendering the hundred responsible for damages done by a mob, is founded on this principle. It is so important, that the reader will, perhaps, pardon another illustration.

Amongst boys as amongst men, a degree of pugnacity exists, to the annoyance of the more quiet portion. This was checked at a certain school by giving full permission to the boys to fight whenever they liked, and at the same time prescribing certain simple rules for the combat, as follows :—

Thus aiding the prevention, the detection, and the punishment of offenders, it renders the interference of the police far less necessary, and when called for, more effective.

§ This principle might perhaps be applied with advantage to the admission under regulations of certain classes of *skilled* workmen by means of tickets, for a limited number of days.

Most effective assistance might be rendered both to the police and to the attendants at the Exposition by the following plan :—Allow a certain

1. When two boys wish to fight, they must inform the chief usher of their wish.
2. He must appoint a time for the combat, not sooner than three, nor more than six hours, after the notice.
3. At the appointed time, if the lads are still desirous of the contest, the chief usher must take the pugnacious ones to an enclosure, where they cannot be seen by their comrades. He then desires them to fight until they are tired, he standing by to see fair play.
4. Any boy present or assisting at an illegal fight will be punished.

The consequence is that their honour or their ill-humour is soon satisfied. No party is made, to back them ; no friends call out to them, "Give it him, Tom !" "At him, Jack !" Their pugnacity is not, as it has been in some instances at public schools, unnaturally excited by the stimulus either of betting or of brandy.

After long experience, it was found that quarrels rarely arrived at a fight. It was the *interest* of all the rest of the school to make some just and amicable arrangement.

number of persons, in whom the executive can repose confidence,—generally master manufacturers or employers,—the privilege of recommending a small number of their best and most regular workmen or assistants, to whom should be granted tickets of admission, subject to the following conditions :—

1. Tickets of admission shall be granted for periods of from three to any greater number of days. Some tickets being for the first three days of each week, or otherwise, as may be convenient.

2. They shall either be gratuitous or obtainable by a small payment.

3. Each ticket-holder shall wear the ticket by a string from the button of his coat, or as may be arranged.

4. He shall, when required by the police or attendants, assist in any duty they may desire for the safety or general convenience of the expositors.

5. Whenever he observes any irregularity, or has reason to believe that thieves or improper persons have obtained admission, he is to inform the nearest policeman.

6. Whenever he observes any machine or any object exhibited, to be out of order, or in danger of being injured, or its parts misplaced, he is to communicate the fact to the nearest attendant, who will refer him to the proper superintendent of that department. He will explain the defect he has

pointed out, and if asked by the superintendent, he is to put it in order, or suggest to him some other person then present, who may be better able to complete the reparation.

7. Each master should be required to pledge his word that he will only recommend trustworthy persons. Each workman admitted might simply be required to give his word of honour that he would assist.

These regulations ought to be printed and stuck up in various parts of the building.

It would, indeed, be desirable to have a certain number of boards placed in the most public parts of the Exposition, on which should be fixed and properly classified all rules, and other information useful to the public. Also notices as to prices and hours of visiting the Exposition might from time to time be affixed. Each board ought also to have a plan of the ground-floor and galleries of the building, on which the names of the different subjects and countries occupying the various parts, might be readily ascertained by the visitors.

CHAPTER XI.

BESIDES those universal advantages which will result, in a greater or less degree, to every nation maintaining friendly intercourse with its neighbours, there are others arising from the Exposition, which may be secured by a little industry and small expense, if timely thought is bestowed upon them.

There are also opportunities for advancing several kindred subjects to which it may be useful to allude.

The most obvious is the facility it will afford of making extensive collections of examples of the present state of many industrial products.* All woven manufactures, for example, might be arranged in books. A small piece of each article being pasted in, might be followed by a short statement of the various facts relating to it—as, for example, a piece of plain cambric—

* The French chamber has devoted 50,000 francs to the purchase of specimens.—(*Illustrated News*, 2d. Feb. 1851.)

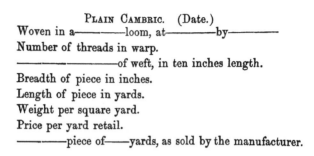

Coloured woven goods might be similarly arranged as regards colour, and the note connected with them ought to contain the name and locality of the dyer, and also the nature of the dye used. Such volumes would hereafter become highly instructive, and save many costly experiments. But it will be necessary to provide against, or to allow for the fading of the colouring matter. This could be done only by preserving some portion of it unchanged by time or exposure. Woven fabrics will not supply this test, but another department of manufacture would, if properly treated, give by the permanence of its colours, invaluable aid not only to many arts, but also to the naturalist and the man of science.

§ The enamel colours used on porcelain, have the permanent character required. Different manufactories excel in different colours. The first step therefore would be to invite each manufacturer to send tablets of porcelain of a given size, on which are to be painted a number of small squares, con-

taining all the pure colours he employs.   Besides
these squares, a certain number of other squares
should contain two or more combinations of these
colours, two by two, or in such proportions as are
usually employed.

The comparison of these tablets would indicate
where the purest and most useful porcelain colours
could be obtained.   The next step would be that
a small committee of manufacturers and men of
science, should decide on the number of combinations and shades of colour it might be desirable to
bring together as permanent and standard objects
of reference.

The different makers of porcelain should then
each receive an order for a certain number of
tablets containing those colours in which they
respectively excel.   Each small square should be
numbered.   A sufficient quantity of the proper
materials constituting each colour, should then be
mixed in the proper proportion, and applied at the
same time, to the same number on each tablet ;
and these tablets should be exposed to the fire
under as nearly as possible the same circumstances
of heat, and for the same length of time.

Thus an extensive system of unchangeable
colours might be obtained, and if 500 sets were
made, they might be distributed in all the great cities
and universities of the world.   It might perhaps
be found that certain colours were deficient, and

this would of course stimulate discovery by making known the want. Thus, in the course of upwards of twenty-five years, during which the author has been collecting on a small scale, such tablets of colours, he has been unable to meet with any specimen of an enamel colour at all approaching to the pure scarlet of the common geranium.

The utility of such sets of standard colours would be very great, enabling all nations to speak a language regarding colour at once accurate and universal. It might serve as the starting point and the test of many analogous collections of materials tinted by colours of more transitory duration, whose relative degree of fixity might thus be measured : as silks, cottons, linens, woollens, leather, paper, and many other materials.

There are two coloured substances which seem to promise a higher degree of permanence than those just mentioned—sealing-wax and glass. For these admit of the renewal of their surfaces by grinding, in case atmospheric or external causes should have altered or impaired the superficial colour.

A collection of small squares of sealing-wax would be cheaper, and might if duly verified by comparison with the porcelain standard be in many cases a useful instrument. Glass also might supply a suit of transparent colours of great interest. A complete collection of the enamel colours used for the mosaic work made at Rome would also be instructive.

§ Perhaps the most important advantage which such an Exposition can confer, is to instruct the consumer in the art of judging of the character of the commodity he is about to purchase. Besides the money we pay in return for the skill, labour, and capital expended in producing each article we purchase; a further, and often a very considerable sum is paid in order to assure us that it possesses those qualities which the vendor has asserted. This is called the *cost of verification;* in some cases, as in that of white sugar, it is very small, for almost every one can see by its external character the degree of goodness of that article. In other cases nothing less than a whole life spent in acquiring a knowledge of his subject, can be of any avail, as *in the case of the purchase of a field.* The verification of the fact that the vendor has really the right to sell it, can, in many cases, be arrived at only by a profound chancery-lawyer, and sometimes requires an expense even beyond the value of the field itself.

When the purchaser has been convinced that he is no judge of the goodness of an article, he usually buys it at some shop having the reputation of selling only the best of the kind. In this case he justly pays a higher price to the vendor, who ought to be remunerated for his skill in selecting good articles from the manufacturer or merchant, and for his integrity in not taking advantage of the ignorance of his customer.

It may be contended that it is cheaper for the purchaser to pay for the use of the skill and integrity of the vendor than to spend his own time in acquiring the same skill; and in many instances this is true. Still, however, the integrity remains to be paid for, and if simple and ready modes of verification were more generally known, a very large portion of this loss of time would be saved.

In all those articles which are easily verified the retail price varies but little; whilst on those that are difficult to verify, the price of the same article, although apparently of the same quality, will be found to vary considerably at different shops.

The duties of the various juries who will examine and recommend the articles for which prizes are to be awarded, will require much consideration. It cannot be expected, even after long experience through several successive expositions, that it would be possible to form a jury which should satisfy every exhibitor. Much, however, may be done, even at the first, by a sincere desire to arrive at just conclusions, and by an earnest endeavour to inform the public of the principles, and to point out the observations, which have led their judgment to the decisions at which they may arrive. Each of the

purely mechanical arts is allied to one or more of
the sciences; almost all their various processes are
amenable to, and explicable by known laws; it is
possible for him who is a perfect master of his own
craft, so to explain them without technical terms,
and in the language of common sense, that most
persons of tolerably liberal education, and possessing a fair average intellect, may not only understand the effect produced, but admire the ingenuity
by which it was attained.

§ It is of great importance that an effort should
be made to remove that veil of mystery which unfortunately, even in minds otherwise well instructed,
often shrouds the principles on which perfection in
manufactures, in science, and still more remarkably
in the fine arts, depends.   These principles nevertheless are founded immutably on the nature of the
material world around us, as well as upon our own
internal feelings.   Those which regulate taste are as
general, although its rules are not so precise, as those
which relate to physics.   Nor need it be dreaded
that a knowledge of the *grounds* of that admiration
which works of genius ever command from cultivated minds, should diminish the pleasure derived
from their contemplation.

Show to the student some mechanism effecting
results apparently beyond the reach of the art, and
he becomes impressed with the immense distance
between his own intelligence and that which con-

trived it. Explain to him the simple means and
the beautiful combinations by which it is effected,
you then raise him in his own estimation, and the studious disciple thus instructed, will ultimately arrive
at the conclusion that the only distance which is
really *immense*, is that existing between the perfection of the highest work of human skill and the
simplest of the productions of nature.

§ In questions relating to taste the subject matter
is so idealized, that the enthusiastic and the timid
equally dread its contact with the more sober
powers of reasoning, lest the process of analysis
should disenchant its visionary scenes, and dissolve
the unreal basis of their delight. Taste the most perfect, without a knowledge of the principles on which
it rests, resembles the barren instinct of animals :
like them, it gathers but little improvement from
experience, and like them it perishes with the extinction of the individual life ; its labours leave no
inheritance to its race.

Taste united with an intimate knowledge of its
principles, and still more if conjoined with the
power of eliminating from the fleeting relations
amongst the objects of its attention, those resemblances which, when sufficiently multiplied and
defined, lead up to the discovery of higher general-
izations, confers upon its enviable possessor a double
source of happiness ; it adds the delight of an intellectual triumph to those romantic feelings which are

excited by the beautiful, the lovely, or the sublime
in Nature, or which are suggested by the most
perfect representations of art.

The comprehension of the cause of our pleasure renders us more acute to perceive those elements which
conduce to its existence, to trace their connexion,
to estimate their amount, to mould into form, and
to call up for the happiness of others and of ourselves, their endless combinations.

There is, however, for that rare union of judgment, imagination, and taste, which we call genius,
when each exists in due proportion and in rich
abundance, a yet higher object, a still nobler ambition. To have given to mankind those models,
which, after twenty centuries, still rivet their attention, commanding unbounded admiration and
defying rivalry, is indeed a splendid achievement, justly repaid by the undying fame which
accompanies the names of those benefactors to
mankind.

But great as undoubtedly our gratitude ought to
be for such gifts, it is trifling compared with that
which civilized society would owe to him, who
should instruct us in the *principles* that guided the
intellect as well as the hands, of those by whom
such immortal works were executed.

In the fine arts, and in the arts of industry, as
well as in the pursuits of science, the highest
department of each is that of the discovery of

principles, and the invention of methods. To in-
vestigate the laws by which human intellect picks
with caution its uncertain track through those
obscure and outlying regions of our knowledge
which separate the known and the certain from
the unknown;—to teach us how to cast as it were
an intellectual and temporary connecting line across
that chasm, by which a new truth is separated from
the old—confident that when arrested by that
isolated truth it will have fixed itself upon one solid
point, amidst a floating chaos of error,—confident
also that, when once the fixity of that single point
has been assured, it is always *possible*, however
formidable the task, to link it by innumerable ties
to established knowledge, and thus to fill up the
intervening space even to the very boundary of its
enlarged domain :— to achieve such a conquest in
any science surpasses all other discoveries, for it
supplies tools for the use of intellect, and enlarges
the limits and the powers of human reason.

§ One of the great advantages of the Exposition
will arise from the interchange of kindly feelings
between the inhabitants of foreign countries and our
own. The classes who visit us will consist neither
of the very elevated nor of the very low. They
will all of them, probably, possess more instruction
and information than the average of their class
amongst their countrymen : consequently they will
consist of persons the most likely to derive instruc-

tion from their visit, and therefore to return home with pleasing impressions.

It has been found on the continent that the periodic unions of men of science have had an excellent effect in removing jealousies and establishing friendships. It has not unfrequently happened that two philosophers have met in such societies, and have entered into discussions which have enabled each to appreciate more justly the talent of the other, before one of them was aware that he had formerly criticised a work of his new friend, in terms which their present good understanding would effectually prevent him from repeating.

The experience we have had of the visit of the National Guard of Paris, strongly confirms this view. It brought out the better feelings of our nature towards our neighbours, and all classes took their share in endeavouring to make those visits agreeable. On their return home, the feeling excited by the visit was conveyed far beyond the actual visitors; and it has left on the population of Paris a permanent advance in good will towards Englishmen.

§ Several objects may be suggested whose discussion would be of the greatest importance for the advancement of the industrial arts, but which are not within the scope of the Exhibition. There are, however, other places of meeting where some of these might be discussed. The Society of Civil Engineers might entertain some inquiries, whilst the Statistical Society would be the most appropriate place for others.

A few of these objects may be shortly alluded to.

§ The law of patents is, perhaps, one of the most interesting as well as of the most difficult questions. Amongst our visitors, doubtless, there will be several who have studied the subject in their own country and who might assist us by their information and experience.

§ We have another law—that of partnership—which presents greater obstacles to the advance of the mechanical arts than even the defective state of the patent law. In England, whoever enters into a partnership, however small a share of the profits he is to receive, yet his whole fortune becomes responsible for any losses. In most other countries there are a class of partnerships called anonymous, or *en commandite*, in which persons willing to risk only a limited sum are entirely relieved of all further responsibility.

The effect of our English system is highly unfavourable to inventors. It prevents in all but a few cases a small capital from being raised by the joint contributions of persons more immediately acquainted with the character and prospects of the inventor, and who are in that respect best fitted to measure the chance of his success.

A far greater impediment, however, arises from its entirely preventing a considerable quantity of capital from being directed to inventions. Its operation may be thus explained.

There exist in this country a great number of persons of manufacturing and commercial habits, whose knowledge of men is considerable, and whose judgment of the capabilities of a proposed scheme or invention, is cautious and judicious.

Persons of this description often possess capital, or such credit as easily to command its use. If partnerships could be entered into, in which the liability was limited, many persons so circumstanced would naturally use their skill and knowledge in selecting a certain number of schemes, in each of which they would embark a small sum. By thus spreading the risks over an extensive field, the profits to the capitalist would be much more certain : whilst many an excellent invention now lost for want of capital to carry it out, would thus enrich its inventor and benefit the country.

§ Connected with the subject of patents is another, which is of some consequence to the public. Many of those capable of improving the arts by new inventions, have no desire to secure their discoveries by patent and thus to render them profitable to themselves, but are willing to give the public the entire advantage.

Now it is supposed that, if an inventor, under the existing law, publishes the drawings of an engine which has not actually been constructed, a machine-maker might make the machine, take out a patent for it, and supply the public to the exclusion even of the inventor himself.

If the invention is a purely mechanical contrivance, it is quite possible with mere drawings and with the aid of the Mechanical Notation to demonstrate the possibility of its construction and of all its movements, with the same certainty as that with which a proposition in Euclid is proved.

It seems then desirable, that some mode of publication should be arranged by which the public should really enjoy the gifts which science may present without risking monopoly by an interloper.

§ The subject of co-operation is one of the greatest importance, and like many other social questions neither its principles nor its limits seem to be clearly understood. It is of the utmost importance that the masses should be enlightened on a subject so exciting, and bearing so directly on their interests. But until it has been further investigated, and numerous instances having a practical connexion with its principles have been collected, it is hopeless to attempt a popular treatment of the subject. It would be highly desirable that those of our foreign visitors who have at all studied that most important question, should communicate to us the results of their experience.

§ The *Mechanical Notation* to which a slight allusion has been made, is a system of signs by which all machinery may be perfectly described even without the necessity of any explanation in words. It forms in fact an universal language, which will be, when generally employed, capable of being read by every people, just as the Arabic numerals are at present.

It has now been in use for more than twenty-five years, during which time many improvements and additions have been made. A considerable portion of it was published in 1826.* Amongst the subsequent additions there is one called the Mechanical Alphabet, which consists of very simple but expressive signs placed above those letters of the alphabet used to express certain parts of machinery. Possibly from 100 to 200 of such signs may be required. Now before any publication is made of those already used, it is of the greatest importance that they should be thoroughly revised, and that practical mechanicians familiar with every branch of the art, should contribute information respecting the requirements in their different departments. Those also who are most experienced in the art of mechanical drawing, ought to confer together respecting the new rules according to which all drawings should have letters attached to the various parts of the machinery they represent.

The *universality of the language* is of such importance, that it would be quite mischievous hastily to publish to the world any other than a well-considered system of signs. The Exposition

* Phil. Trans. 1826, p. 250.

of 1851 furnishes an opportunity for such a re-
vision.

§ Considerable discussion has arisen respecting
the ultimate fate of the Crystal Palace. Three questions have been agitated :—

1. Shall it be pulled down?

2. Shall it be removed to another locality?

3. To what uses can the building be applied if
it is retained?

Public opinion has undergone a great revolution
since the opening of the Exhibition; but however
strongly it may now be expressed, it ought not to
interfere with public faith. If, after all the pro-
testations and pledges of the Commission, that
the building was to be of temporary duration, it
should be permitted to remain permanently in its
present locality, little faith will be given in future
to the promises of public bodies. The pledge contained in the document by which the Commission
was appointed, viz. that 20,000*l.* should be given
in prizes, has neither been redeemed nor forgotten;
and the treatment of the income-tax by the successive
political parties has added little to the respect with
which official promises are regarded.

If the country had originally maintained its un-
doubted right to use its own parks for its own
purposes, the building might then have remained;
but the inhabitants of Belgravia, having raised a
violent opposition to the selection of that locality,

were only pacified on receiving the strongest assurances that the building should be removed after it had fulfilled its original purpose. In justice therefore to them, it must be taken down.

The second question, Shall the Crystal Palace be removed? is by no means decided by the answer given to the first. It would be perfectly consistent with good faith to remove it to any other part of the park not contiguous to Belgrave Square.

The third question, therefore, To what uses can the building be applied? must now be examined, in order to arrive at a definitive decision upon the second.

A wish seems to be very generally entertained for the preservation of the building; and various uses have been suggested to which it might be advantageously applied.

Mr. Paxton wishes to convert it into a winter garden.

M. Gambardella, in his highly interesting pamphlet, " What shall we do with the Glass Palace?" * has proposed to have within its walls alternately exhibitions of painting and of sculpture.

Permanent galleries of the fine arts have also been proposed.

Collections of the industrial arts, and models, have also been suggested.

A portion of it might also be appropriated to the

* Published by Aylott and Jones, Paternoster Row.

building of several theatres for lectures, of various sizes, capable of containing from 100 to 2,000 persons.

The great principle to be borne in mind is, that, whatever the future destination of the building, it must be self-supporting. The best and most certain test of its utility to the public is furnished by the fact of their being willing to pay for the enjoyments it affords them.

The plan of having a considerable portion of the building devoted to a winter garden would supply a great want in our wet and uncertain climate. The temperature ought not to be high, so that exercise might be taken under shelter. No dogs, horses, or carriages ought to be admitted.

A large portion of those residing in the immediate neighbourhood would subscribe, and also many who possessed carriages. But the number of subscribers would depend chiefly on the position chosen for the building. In its *present* locality, the prejudices of the wealthier class would be increased by the injustice of retaining it in violation of the strongest pledges, and it would probably have a very limited number of subscribers.

Perhaps it might be desirable to add reading-rooms for newspapers and for the periodical literature of the day. Subscriptions to these might be either for limited periods, or even for a single day. A refreshment-room, also, would be required.

If, however, the building were removed to the situation proposed in the seventh chapter of this volume, it would be accessible to a much larger number of subscribers. Its two ends being then placed at a small distance from the two great thoroughfares passing Hyde Park Corner and the Marble Arch, a large number of its visitors would arrive by the omnibuses which pass each of those well-frequented localities.

Space might readily be found either for periodical or permanent galleries of painting and of sculpture. An objection has been made to the former, namely, that the light in the glass palace is not fit for the exhibition of paintings. It is singular that it should not have occurred to such objectors that this is almost the only building in which, from its very nature, there exists the most unlimited control over both the quantity and the direction of light that may be required.

The profit to be derived from this part of the establishment will, as in the former questions, depend greatly on the situation of the building.

Another plan, mentioned in the first edition of this work, was, to have collections of the produce and manufactures exhibited on the present occasion. Few applications of the building would be more appropriate, and scarcely any could be more useful, than this. Fortunately, the Executive Committee have undertaken the task, and it cannot be doubted that the exhibitors will willingly lighten their labour by giving every assistance in their power. One or two suggestions may here be offered, for the purpose of impressing on the exhibitors at future Expositions the great importance of attaching to each object a brief and condensed account of facts connected with it. In the article of raw materials there will not be much difficulty, as there are many instances of excellence in that department. The case of drugs from Liverpool is a good illustration. Their price, however, is omitted, because it was forbidden. In the permanent collection, this most important element will, of course, occupy its proper place. It might also be useful to give the date of the first importation of each drug, and the first application to its various uses. The quantity, also, of the chemical element on which its use is founded contained in a given weight of the substance would, if known, be highly interesting: as, for instance, the quantity of quinine in a given weight of bark.

In making a collection of machines, there is some fear of occupying a very large space without a corresponding advantage. A lace frame, making in one breadth of fifteen feet from sixty to a hundred repetitions of the same lace, would, commercially speaking, be the most advantageous; but such a frame with only ten repetitions would be more useful for instruction. The various self-acting mules, also, would easily fill a large room. Perhaps the collection might be confined to working models: these might be made, from time to time, to replace the larger machines, and funds for that purpose might be derived from the payments of the visitors both to the exhibition and to the lectures which ought to be given to explain the collection.

In making a collection of specimens of manufactured articles, as well as of produce, it would in many cases add little to the expense if a sufficient quantity were purchased to divide into many samples. Thus, the collections of foreign countries and of our own cities might be enriched by authentic specimens. This view applies more particularly to collections of woven fabrics.

A well authenticated collection of cotton, flax, wool, and silk, in the raw state, through all their successive stages of manufacture, up to the woven fabrics of which they constitute the basis, if accompanied by the prices of each at intervals of ten years during the last century, would furnish materials of the most valuable kind, and would greatly aid the economist, the statesman, and the philosopher, in discovering and putting to the test the principles connected with their several inquiries.

It is not necessary, or even desirable, that this collection should consist of articles of fancy: it ought to be composed of all those fabrics which, although at first rare and costly, have ultimately

L

become objects of habitual consumption by large classes of the community.

Another purpose of great importance to which a portion of such a building might be applied, is the construction of convenient theatres for the delivery of lectures, and for the discussion of questions of interest. The want of such buildings in the western part of the metropolis has long been felt, and acts injuriously on the progress of knowledge.

In the present state of society, oral statements of the great principles which govern it, illustrated by striking facts drawn with judgment from varied sources, would, if delivered with ability and good taste, attract large audiences. Even science itself might be rendered popular by such means. Yet if any highly gifted person, qualified for such a task, were willing to devote to the subject the time necessary to assure the success of his efforts, he would now be stopped at the very threshold, for he could find no convenient theatre in any part of the west of London, which he could hire for the delivery of such a course of lectures.

The only theatre capable of holding 1,000 persons, is that of the Royal Institution in Albemarle Street. Let us suppose the lecturer capable of attracting 1,000 subscribers, each willing to pay a sovereign for a short course of lectures. How would the sum thus raised be divided? He could lecture at that theatre only by the permission

of the Managers, who would scarcely pay him more
than 100*l*.¹ for the course. The 1,000*l*. therefore,
which the public would willingly pay for the
instruction they received would be thus divided:—

To the intellect which charmed them . . . £100
To the rent of the room in which they listened. 900
                                            _____
                                            £1,000
                                            _____

If the 900*l*. were the remuneration of the creative
mind, and the 100*l*. were the payment for the use
of the room and the necessary attendants, the
information of several classes of society would be
far other than it now is, and the status of the
lecturer would be entirely altered. At present,
however great the talent of the instructor, his
position is not exactly that which the interests of
society demand. The term, *itinerant* lecturer,
has long been one of reproach, and even now it
is not thought quite dignified in a gentleman to
give a lecture *for money*. The reason is obvious :
nothing is thought respectable in England which
does not produce wealth. Any shrewd and unscrupulous fellow, who swindles on a gigantic
scale, will, if he succeed, be immediately received
with welcome into what is called the best society.
Neither wit nor talent are necessary for his admission : if, indeed, he be horridly vulgar, a few

(1) It is far from the author's intention to reproach in the
slightest degree the Managers of that most valuable Institution.
Every member having a right to be present at every lecture,
it is not in their power to do otherwise.

L 2

additional hundreds of thousands will procure him absolution in fashionable eyes, even for that most deadly sin.

Enable the instructor to receive his due portion of that reward which the public are willing to pay, and he too will become rich, and therefore eminently respectable. With this increased remuneration, minds of a higher order will be attracted to the study of the most difficult of arts,—that of teaching; and the time will arrive when accomplished, enlightened, and independent men may earn from five to ten thousand a-year without courting a constituency for parliamentary influence, or a minister for justice to merit he is incapable of appreciating.

Such results, however, demand the use of convenient theatres of various sizes, placed in situations easily accessible.

It appears then that, on every ground which has been considered, the utility of the Crystal Palace will depend almost entirely on the situation chosen for its ultimate position.

Looking at the question in a purely commercial view, considering the difficulty of access from the north to its present locality; contrasting it with the facility of access from every quarter in the site proposed; it is not too much to presume that its revenue would be so greatly enlarged by the removal, that it would justify an expenditure of forty or even of fifty thousand pounds.

CHAPTER XII.

SEVERAL causes have justly lowered the position of science in England. The conduct of the Royal Society, and of men of science themselves, has equally contributed to this result. In a work on the Decline of Science* in 1830, I exposed the wretched mismanagement of the Royal Society, but not until in conjunction with Wollaston and other eminent men, I had found the inutility of every effort we made to improve it from within. Our reform bill stands recorded upon the minutes of the coun- cil, with the signatures of Wollaston, of Young, of Herschel, and of others whose names ought to have commanded respect: but it was defeated by an in- genious manœuvre.

The facts stated in the work alluded to, have never been disputed: one answer† only having, as far as

---

* Reflections on the Decline of Science in England, and on some of its Causes. 1830.

† A small pamphlet, the production of an amiable and excellent foreign philosopher, cannot be considered an answer : since it did not *contradict* the facts, and only answered opinions on science, which were *not* maintained in that book.

I am aware, ever been attempted to any part of that volume. It appeared in the Annals of Philosophy, and was first mentioned to me by the late Francis Baily, F.R.S. Not having then seen it, I inquired whether he thought any reply necessary; his answer was, "*No: it is a full admission of the truth of your statement.*"

§ In France the body who elect to offices in the Institute, are men of the highest intellectual attainments, whose suffrage it is an honour to receive, and who, during the existence of the monarchy, constituted one amongst the classes out of whom Peers of France were selected.

In England, out of about 800 Fellows of the Royal Society, the greater part of them know nothing of science, and of course their votes swamp those of the members most competent to pronounce opinions. The new mode of admitting fellows of the Royal Society, has had a good effect in improving the qualification of those admitted; but unfortunately, its operation is so slow that it will be many years before the Society is relieved from its incumbrances.

§ In the Academy of Sciences at Paris, the office of Secretary is an object of ambition even to men of the highest scientific attainments. It is usually held by persons of the greatest eminence, who are themselves at the same time carrying out original inquiries on subjects connected with their official

duties. It is sufficient to cite the names of De-
lambre, of Fourier, of Cuvier, and of Arago.

In England the Secretary of the Royal Society
of London occupies no such position. To some of
our most eminent men, it may, when young, have
been an object of ambition to hold it for a few years :
but considering the very moderate pay of 100*l*.
a-year, and how considerable a portion of time must
be occupied by its duties if conscientiously fulfilled,
it is rare that any man of original talent and independent feeling will join in the intrigues by which
it is too frequently obtained.

In consequence of this state of things, the
officers of the Royal Society are most frequently
third or fourth-rate men, who not having sufficient
occupation in their own professions, seek the office
as a means of adding to their income. Or, they may
be, in some cases, military men, who being paid by
the public for other duties, are glad to get relieved
from them without the loss of their emoluments.
Persons holding offices in the Royal Society ought
by their scientific eminence to confer dignity on
their office : instead of acquiring a position in the
world by its acceptance.

§ Again, the justice of the decisions of the Council
in awarding their medals, has been publicly im-
peached. A very few years since, a general meeting
of the Society was summoned on the requisition of
several of its members, to inquire into the circum-

stances attending the award of certain Royal medals. It was admitted by the President that there had been considerable irregularities in some of the awards, and the Council only escaped a vote of censure in consequence of some little want of management in those who proposed it.

During this discussion one of the Fellows of the Royal Society got up, and remarked that although this case was very bad, it became trifling when compared with the circumstances attending the very first award of the Royal medals ; for on that occasion the Council had wilfully violated the laws they had themselves established for their distribution, and that on his formally demonstrating the facts by reference to their own minutes, they with singular consistency refused to alter their unfair and unjust decision.

§ Difficulties of another kind arise respecting the Presidents of Societies. When the office of President is really or practically a permanent one, it is very difficult to carry on the business of the Society if the President is a person of exalted rank, or if he do not permanently reside in London.

In either case it usually happens that a secretary or treasurer, or other officer who is resident, insensibly becomes the means of communication with the President, who is naturally anxious to be acquainted with the feelings and wishes of the body over which he presides. The most honest officer can scarcely fail to have some little bias towards his own opinions : he will naturally mix more with those who approve of, than with those who differ from them, and will consequently, although perhaps unintentionally, communicate to the President a one-sided view of his own, as the dominant opinion of the Society.

The President, on the other hand, however really anxious he may be to introduce any amendments which he conceives advantageous for the Society, will naturally doubt their policy if informed that they are not in unison with the opinions of the body. He will communicate with his treasurer, secretary, or other officer, and almost always express his concurrence in the course proposed to him as being the most agreeable to the body at large.

The officer, receiving such a reply, will naturally mention at the Council the opinions of the President. He may even from good nature allow the Council to think that the President himself *originated* the views he only *adopted* because he believed them to be those of the Society.

Under such circumstances, it is difficult to oppose the expressed wishes of the absent President, and strangely enough, without any intentional deceit, President, Council, and Society are supposed to be unanimous in doing what each by itself thinks inexpedient.

§ It is true that by great kindness, good sense,

and decision of character, the Prince or absent
President may in some cases mitigate or prevent
these evils. Such cases, however, are the exception, not the rule.

§ In a work containing views on the state of
science in England, foreigners at least will expect
that I should take some notice of my own calculating engines.

I had hoped that the history of the transactions
between myself and the government respecting them,
as related in the eleventh chapter of the History of
the Royal Society by Mr. Weld, together with the
two criticisms on that work in the Athenæum,*
would have rendered any further explanation on
my part unnecessary. Many persons, however,
who admit these as fully explaining the part I was
compelled to take, have at the same time expressed
to me their doubts that some occult agency was at
work to prejudice the government, and have asked
who were its scientific advisers on such an important subject, during the long period in which the
Difference Engine was in abeyance.

§ I have not been blind to the passions and interests of men. My own pursuits were of such a
character that they interfered with those of none of
my colleagues in the paths of science ; and perhaps
I may have trusted too much to this circumstance
as exempting me from rivalry and jealousy.

* Athenæum, 14 Oct. 1848, and 16 Dec. 1848.

As a reformer both in science and in politics, I knew that I should excite enmity in the minds of some honest men, and also in those of many other persons who dreaded inquiry into jobs not yet exposed. When I published the Decline of Science, in 1830, I certainly was not aware how many would include themselves in the latter class: but had I foreseen it, I should not have altered my course. To have met and to have defeated intrigue by watchfulness, might not have been a difficult task, but it would have required too great a sacrifice of time devoted to far higher objects. It was, moreover, an occupation for which I had little taste.

The time, however, has now arrived when, having given up all expectation of constructing the Analytical Engine from the drawings which I had caused to be made at very great expense, I think it right to state the result of my own observations, and especially to point out the facts that have come to light to confirm them. These, if they do not open the eyes of some, who, having been themselves deceived, have done me injustice, will at all events be of use for the future, and may save the young and inexperienced enthusiast of science from embarking in undertakings, honourable to the country, but ruinous to himself.

It has often been remarked, that an event in itself trivial sometimes leads to results with which it seems to have no conceivable connexion.

A beaver constructing his dwelling on the plateau of the Andes, may have turned the course of a river, which otherwise would shortly have joined the Pacific, into a valley through which, after lengthened wanderings, it now flows into the Atlantic Ocean.

So, by some strange combination of circumstances, a quarrel in which I had no part, and with whose origin I am unacquainted, seems to have had an unanticipated effect in impeding the construction of the Calculating Engines.

At the time of the foundation of the Astronomical Society, Sir James South, whose observatory and whose house were hospitably open to every cultivator of astronomy, was on terms of intimate friendship with almost all of those persons at that period most eminent in science. It is sufficient to mention the names of Wollaston and Davy, and to add that when the late Mr. Fallows was appointed Astronomer at the Cape, although previously a stranger, he became for several months the guest of Sir James South, who assisted him in acquiring that practical knowledge of instruments so necessary in his new avocation.*

§ In 1829 Sir James South was elected President

---

* Sir James South, in conjunction with Sir John Herschel, completed the examination of 380 double and triple stars ; a work for which the authors were awarded the great Astronomical prize of the Institute of France in 1825, and the Medal of the Astronomical Society of London in 1826.

of the Astronomical Society.   It now appears, however, that previously to this appointment, *a party
had been formed* adverse to Sir J. South, which
party, with the view of thwarting him, placed in
the office of Secretary the Rev. Richard Sheepshanks, Fellow of Trinity Coll., Cambridge.*

In March, 1831, the Board of Visitors of the
Royal Observatory of Greenwich, met at the Admiralty, to consider the propriety of separating the
duties of Superintendent of the Nautical Almanac
from those of Astronomer Royal.   The new arrangement was advocated, amongst others, by Sir J. South,
and after some discussion, in which Capt. Beaufort
and myself took part, it was ultimately carried.   As
we were leaving the meeting-room, Mr. Sheepshanks addressing me said : " I am determined to
" put down Sir James South, and if you and other
" respectable men will give him your support, I
" will put you down."   He at the same time told
me he " intended to put Captain Beaufort down."

During the course of 1832, it was found that
the large equatorial mounting which had been contrived and executed by Troughton, for his friend
Sir J. South's twelve-inch object-glass, was an
entire failure.   This produced at the time a difference between two friends who esteemed each other
highly, and who had been for years united by

* " When he [Sir J. S.] was elected President, I [Rev. R. S.]
was elected Secretary to keep him in order."

reciprocal acts of kindness in ties of "*very inti-mate*" friendship.   Well acquainted myself with
the character of the parties, and the circumstances
of the case, I have not the slightest doubt that this
unfortunate affair might easily, by the exertions of
judicious friends, have terminated in the entire
restoration of their former friendship.   But this
was a course which the Rev. R. Sheepshanks took
effectual means to prevent.   Having himself a
"*personal*" quarrel with Sir James South, he
"*offered*" his services to assist Messrs. Troughton
and Simms.   He "*offered to go*" himself to exa-mine the instrument in Sir J. South's observa-tory, and "*got his friend, Professor Airy, to go with
him*" for the purpose of remedying the defects of
the Equatorial.

Notwithstanding he was told by Mr. Simms that
"*Sir J. South had declared that no person could
have been pitched upon more obnoxious than your-self,*" he still persevered in obtruding himself
into Sir J. South's observatory as the agent of
Troughton and Simms, until it was at last dis-covered that no after contrivances or expense could
correct the errors of an instrument itself radically
defective in principle.

It may readily be supposed that the continuance
for months of these visits by Mr. Sheepshanks and
Professor Airy, and the *irritating correspondence*
consequent upon them, which, though *nominally*

that of Troughton and Simms, was really "*directed by*" the Rev. R. Sheepshanks, destroyed all hope of a reconciliation. The parties then had recourse to the Court of King's Bench, and it was curious to observe the vigour and energy with which the Rev. R. Sheepshanks applied himself to the exercise of his earlier studies.*

Having *volunteered* his services to Messrs. Troughton and Simms—he "*wrote every letter*" for them during the subsequent law-suit—he acted for them in all the various characters of "*friend*" and "*adviser*"—of "*workman*" and "*agent*"—of "*attorney*" and "*counsel*;" †—he made an "*affidavit*" in the case—became a *witness* himself—and undertook to *intimidate witnesses* on the opposite side.

This latter performance is fortunately rare in England, and is so remarkable that it is necessary to give some account of the proceedings.

Not wishing to become involved in so disagreeable a case, I had refused to be a witness on the part of Sir J. South. Having, however, had some conversation on the subject with the late Lord Abinger (then Mr. Scarlett), he represented to me that my evidence was essential for the justice of the

* At an earlier period of his life, his studies were directed towards the profession of the law.

† On the 19th July, 1836, at the 23d meeting under the Arbitrator, the Rev. R. Sheepshanks *cross-examined* Mr. Savage the Architect.

case, and upon that ground I reluctantly waived my objection to appear as a witness.

Having been examined in chief on the seventeenth day of the Arbitration, I remained in the room a few minutes after the Arbitrator had left it. The Rev. R. Sheepshanks, the only other person then present, addressing me said, " it was necessary " to *discredit me* because I had supported Sir J. " South." He added that " he would, at a future " time, *attack me* publicly on *another subject,* on " account of the part I had taken in this matter."

The remembrance of his former threats more than four years before at the Visitation at the Admiralty, added to the knowledge of the unremitting perseverance with which he had carried on his hostility to Sir J. South, satisfied me that it would be unsafe for the cause of truth, and possibly injurious to myself, if I were not to take measures for making known the nature of the weapons which the Rev. R. Sheepshanks was employing. As he had ventured, *after* my having given evidence on oath, to threaten me with injury, with the hope of inducing me to modify that evidence on cross-examination, it appeared to me probable that he might have been tampering with the evidence of other witnesses in the same cause, who from their position or circumstances in life, might be compelled by the fear of his vengeance to shape their evidence so as to adapt it to his views.

The Rev. R. Sheepshanks discovered on reflection no impropriety in this course of intimidating witnesses, or of attacking those who could not be induced to take up his own private quarrels. He thus defended both.

" *I think it allowable to throw down the gauntlet* " *in this manner.*"

" *I have another ground of dispute with Captain* "*Beaufort, and certainly intend to put him down.*"

The gallant Admiral has survived many a dangerous day, and needs not the pen of a friend to protect his honest and well-earned fame.

The reader may perhaps be astonished at the statement made in the preceding pages, and feel disposed to consider it an *ex parte* statement. It *is entirely* an *ex parte* statement : it is not necessary for its support that the reader should give credence even to that small part of it which appears to rest on my own evidence before the Arbitrator. *The whole of it is founded entirely on the testimony of the* Rev. R. Sheepshanks *himself.* Every statement of those which are marked as quotations was either elicited from him on his cross-examination, or in the few instances in which it came from myself, its correctness was confirmed by his subsequent admission or re-statement. After my statement, and the Rev. R. Sheepshanks' reply to it, the Arbitrator addressing him said—

" With respect to the matter of fact, you agree?"

M

Rev. R. Sheepshanks.   " Yes, we agree as to the " matter of fact."

Professor Airy, who was afterwards appointed Astronomer Royal, had long before become as deeply engaged as his friend Mr. Sheepshanks in this most unfortunate quarrel. Years of aggravating delay and discussion resulted from the procrastinated reference, and at length one of the parties, Mr. Troughton, being dead, a decision not satisfactory to either was given in December 1838.   But the inextinguishable desire " to put down Sir James South" survived the lawsuit which was only used as a means, and reappeared from time to time through the aid of the press, in forcible but somewhat unmeasured charges and recriminations between the Astronomer Royal, the Rev. R. Sheepshanks and others on the one side, and the astronomer of Campden Hill on the other.

It was a curious though a very painful study, to observe from time to time the various consequences of this feud.

Against those men of science who refused to forsake their ancient social relations with Sir James South, a system of disparagement was maintained which could not fail in the course of time to produce its effects.   The avowed object of the party of which the Rev. R. Sheepshanks was the organ, was, in his own expressive words, to *discredit and put down every respectable person* who supported Sir J. South.

It was melancholy to observe the gradual change in the expression of opinions by some of those qualified from their knowledge to guide the opinion of the public. Intimidated at first into silence; the uncontradicted assertions of those around them then got possession of their minds, until at length, without any new examination, they were flattered into an acquiescence in, if not indeed into the expression of, opinions entirely opposite to their former ones. These new views were doubtless conveyed by their flatterers to other ears, and thus the process of "*discrediting every respectable person*" opposed to them, was carried on under the authority of honourable names.

One after another almost all Sir James South's old friends and acquaintance amongst *men of science only, however,* were alienated from him.

One man was alarmed by the fear that some inaccuracies in his astronomical publications should be severely criticised. Of another it was hinted that his mathematics were all wrong, and might be shown up.

Those who were timid feared the anger of the dominant party; those who were young might have their prospects blighted by even appearing in friendly relations with him who supported the unequal conflict; those who were old loved repose, and found it easiest to appear to side with the most numerous party; whilst those who saw

through the whole of it, had better things where-
with to occupy their minds, than to attend to such
affairs.

It is obvious to all who have observed society
that such a system of "*discrediting*" carried on for
a series of years, especially against one too much
occupied or too proud to expose it, must end in
establishing the set of opinions propagated by the
party. Honest and even tolerably well-informed
persons, will at length be misled, and be found to
adopt them.

Opinions thus propagated must have had their
influence widely spread, and unless those members
of the various administrations with whom decisions
relative to the Difference Engine rested, had been
either highly skilled in mathematical science, or
deeply read in human nature, it would have been
almost impossible for them not to have been
misled.

The former qualification is unnecessary; the
latter is indispensable for a statesman. Of the
eight Prime-ministers with whom I have had communications relative to the Difference Engine, *one*
only personally examined it; doubtless not with
the view of criticising the mechanism, but of reading the character of its author. Had my *official*
intercourse with that eminent man commenced
earlier or continued later, the fate of the Calculating
Engines would probably have been far different.

It is always difficult to trace intriguers up to a direct intercourse with government. In the present case, the vanity of some of them overcame their judgment, and they gave themselves out as advisers of the government on scientific subjects. To these I shall not at present refer, but confine myself to citing from official documents two cases of direct communication with the government by persons on whose judgment it appears to have relied.

The Whigs seemed to have had great confidence in the devotion of the Rev. R. Sheepshanks to their interests, since they took the extraordinary step of appointing him, although a Clergyman, one of the Boundary Commissioners under the Reform Bill, and he is, I believe, at present one of the Standard Measure Commission.

The Astronomer Royal, besides his situation at Greenwich, has been a member of several Commissions :—

The Tidal Harbour Commission.
The Standard Measure Commission.
The Harbour of Refuge Commission.
The Railway Gauge Commission.

The following are extracts from his Annual Reports :—

" The Board of Admiralty, on my representation of the in-
" terruption to our business caused by the rating of so many
" Chronometers, and *by my own employment on public business*
" *unconnected with the Observatory,* immediately sanctioned

the employment of an additional computer."—*Astron. Royal, Rep. June* 1841, p. 7.

" On former occasions I have avowed without scruple that " I do not consider the Royal Observatory as a mere isolated " place for the conduct of Astronomical observations. I consider " it a part, perhaps the most important part, of the scientific " institutions of this country."—P. 18.

" In concluding this long report, I have been uniformly supported by the *confidence of the government.*" — *Astron. Royal, Rep. June* 1844, p. 20.

The following extract of a letter from the Astronomer Royal to the late Sir Robert Peel, shows that his time was so occupied with the labours of the Railway Gauge Commission, that he was unable to draw up a memorial which he had him-self proposed, even though it related to an astronomical subject—our colonial observatories.

*   *   *   * " I have been so closely employed on the papers of the Railway Gauge Commission, that it has been impossible for me to draw up a memorial before the present time. *   *   *   *

" April 16th, 1846.

" To the Right Hon. Sir Robert Peel, Bart., &c."

" By the giving opinions on subjects of railways and *other mechanical matters referred to me by Government*, it has appeared that our energies are not wholly absorbed in the mere Astronomy of the Observatory."—*Astron. Royal, Rep. June* 1846, p. 10.

(N.B. The italics do not occur in the original quotations.)

Now it is evident from these extracts from Reports of the Astronomer Royal to the Board of Visitors and from other facts, that he wishes himself to be considered the general referee of Government in all scientific questions.

The office of Astronomer Royal is one of great importance: it requires the undivided energy and talents of one person, and great as Mr. Airy's abilities undoubtedly are, yet it is highly injudicious to divert them from their legitimate object,—the direction of the many arduous duties of the establishment over which he presides.

During many years I have frequently found, in my communications with members of Government on subjects connected with the Calculating Engines, difficulties on their part which remained entirely unexplained;—unseen obstacles which were never alluded to, but whose existence could not be doubted.

Although frequently warned by personal friends that it was unwise to neglect such machinations as those which I have, at length, been reluctantly compelled to expose; yet I was unwilling for a long time to believe that they were directed against myself.

I have now traced the connexion of the Rev. R. Sheepshanks, (who had avowed his determination " *to discredit me,*" and also to " *attack me on another subject at a future time,*") through his friend the Astronomer Royal, with the Government. According to the Astronomer Royal's own statement, he was their adviser on all scientific subjects. The

Government had no other official adviser, and would scarcely have ventured to decide upon points connected with some of the most profound questions of mathematics, on their own responsibility.

There are, I am aware, other channels than those of official reports, by which the Government may have been influenced. I do not, therefore, expect to find any formal report denying the practical utility of the Calculating Engines, or the possibility of constructing them.

If there is any such, I claim as a matter of justice, that it be published. The Difference Engine and the Analytical Engine, are questions of pure science. If the Astronomer Royal has maintained that they are either useless or impracticable, then the grounds of that opinion *must* have been stated, and, if published, the solidity of those grounds might be examined.

It now becomes necessary to take a very brief review of the conduct of Government with respect to the Difference Engine. Having contrived and executed a small model of a Difference Engine, I published a very short account of it in a letter to Sir Humphry Davy, in the year 1822. At the wish of the Government I undertook to construct for them an engine on a much larger scale, which should print its results. I continued to work at this Engine until 1834, refusing in the mean time other sources of profitable occupation, amongst which was an office of about 2,500*l.* a-year. Circumstances over which I had no control then caused the work to be suspended.

After eight years of repeated applications, and of the most harassing delay, at the end of 1842 the Government arrived at the resolution of giving up the completion of the Difference Engine, on the alleged ground of its expense.

In the mean time, new views had opened out to me the prospect of performing purely algebraic operations by means of mechanism. To arrive at so entirely unexpected a result I deemed worthy of any sacrifice, and accordingly spared no expense in procuring every subsidiary assistance which could enable me to attain it. Each successive difficulty was met by new contrivances, and at last I found that I had surmounted all the great difficulties of the question, and had made drawings of each distinct department of the Analytical Engine.

Having expended upwards of 20,000*l.* on the experiments and inquiries which had led me to these results, it would not have been prudent to attempt the *construction* of such an engine. I thought, however, that there were several offices in the appointment of Government for which I was qualified, and to which, under the circumstances, I had some claim. I hoped if I had obtained one of these, by fulfilling its laborious duties for a few years, and by allowing the whole salary to accumu-

late, that I might then have been able to retire, and
adding the money thus earned to my own private
resources, that I might yet have enough of life and
energy left to *execute* the Analytical Engine, and
thus complete one of the great objects of my
ambition.

Having neither asked nor been offered any
acknowledgment for all the sacrifices I had made,
I felt that I had some just claims to one of these
appointments. Every application was unsuccessful;
whatever may have been the reasons, the conduct
of Government has been exactly that which might
have been expected had they been the *allies* or the
dupes of the party which thought it necessary,
from enmity to Sir James South, to " discredit"
the author of the Analytical Engine.

One only of the many reports which were circulated, I thought it worth while to contradict, and
that cost me more trouble, and wasted more of my
time, than the refutation of the calumny was worth.
It was boldly and perseveringly stated that I had
received from the Government a large pecuniary
reward for my services.   The fact was, not merely
that I never *did* receive any such reward, but that
I was almost constantly *advancing money* to pay
the engineer who was constructing the Engine for
the Government, before I had myself received the
amount of his bills from the Treasury.

On tracing up these rumours, they were usually

found to arise from a species of dishonesty very difficult to convict. Thus one person circulated them widely; when asked for the grounds of the charge, he referred to certain Parliamentary Papers, and affected to believe that the sums paid *for the workmen* were paid to the *inventor :* of course *he* could no longer safely propagate the falsehood. Another then took up the tale, until he was met by the same question, when *he* not only expressed his delight at being informed of the truth, but half convinced his indignant, though credulous auditor, that *he* would assist in propagating the correction. Thus the assertion was continually repeated, until honourable and upright men, who had been deceived and discovered the deception, were so frequent in society, that it became dangerous to the character of the traducers to continue the circulation of the calumny.

Even since the first edition of this work has appeared, one of these calumnies has been again revived, in the statement that—

The reason why the Government gave up the construction of the original Difference Engine was, that Mr. Babbage refused to finish *it*, and wished them to take up the Difference Engine No. 2.

An attempt has been made to prove its truth by a quotation from this volume, in which the accuser, mistaking dates, assigns the drawings of the Difference Engine No. 2, which did not exist until 1847, as the causes of the discontinuance of No. 1, which was given up in 1843.   This charge too is made in the face of a distinct denial by Mr. Babbage that the late Sir Robert Peel could have been influenced by any such *supposed* wish, because he had in his possession a written *disavowal* of it from Mr. B. himself; it is also made in the teeth of the very words used by the Chancellor of the Exchequer, who, in his letter to Mr. B. regretting the necessity of giving it up, assigns as its cause "*the expense.*"   Both these latter statements had been already published in 1848.

CHAPTER XIII.

CALCULATING ENGINES.

It is not a bad definition of *man* to describe him as a *tool-making animal*. His earliest contrivances to support uncivilized life, were tools of the simplest and rudest construction. His latest achievements in the substitution of machinery, not merely for the skill of the human hand, but for the relief of the human intellect, are founded on the use of tools of a still higher order.

The successful construction of all machinery depends on the perfection of the tools employed, and whoever is a master in the art of tool-making possesses the key to the construction of all machines.

The Crystal Palace, and all its splendid contents, owe their existence to *tools* as the physical means: —to intellect as the guiding power, developed equally on works of industry or on objects of taste.

The contrivance and the construction of tools, must therefore ever stand at the head of the industrial arts.

The next stage in the advancement of those arts

is equally necessary to the progress of each. It is the art of drawing. Here, however, a divergence commences: the drawings of the artist are entirely different from those of the mechanician. The drawings of the latter are Geometrical projections, and are of vast importance in all mechanism. The resources of mechanical drawing have not yet been sufficiently explored: with the great advance now making in machinery, it will become necessary to assist its powers by practical yet philosophical rules for expressing still more clearly by signs and by the letters themselves the mutual relations of the parts of a machine.

As we advance towards machinery for more complicated objects, other demands arise, without satisfying which our further course is absolutely stopped. It becomes necessary to see at a glance, not only every *successive* movement of each amongst thousands of different parts, but also to scrutinize all contemporaneous actions. This gave rise to the Mechanical Notation, a language of signs, which, although invented for one subject, is of so comprehensive a nature as to be applicable to many. If the whole of the facts relating to a naval or military battle were known, the mechanical notation would assist the description of it quite as much as it would that of any complicated engine.

This brief sketch has been given partly with the view of more distinctly directing attention to an important point in which England excels all other countries—the art of *contriving and making tools;* an art which has been continually forced upon my own observation in the contrivance and construction of the Calculating Engines.

When the first idea of inventing mechanical means for the calculation of all classes of astronomical and arithmetical tables, occurred to me, I contented myself with making simple drawings, and with forming a small model of a few parts. But when I understood it to be the wish of the Government that a large engine should be constructed, a very serious question presented itself for consideration :—

Is the present state of the art of making machinery sufficiently advanced to enable me to execute the multiplied and highly complicated movements required for the Difference Engine?

After examining all the resources of existing workshops, I came to the conclusion that, in order to succeed, it would become necessary to advance the art of construction itself. I trusted with some confidence that those studies which had enabled me to contrive mechanism for new wants, would be equally useful for the invention of new tools, or of other methods of employing the old.

During the many years the construction of the Difference Engine was carried on, the following course was adopted. After each drawing had been

made, a new inquiry was instituted to determine
the mechanical means by which the several parts
were to be formed.   Frequently sketches, or new
drawings, were made, for the purpose of constructing the tools or mechanical arrangements thus
contrived.   This process often elicited some simpler
mode of construction, and thus the original contrivances were improved.   In the mean time, many
workmen of the highest skill were constantly
employed in making the tools, and afterwards in
using them for the construction of parts of the
engine.   The knowledge thus acquired by the
workmen, matured in many cases by their own
experience, and often perhaps improved by their
own sagacity, was thus in time disseminated widely
throughout other workshops.   Several of the most
enlightened employers and constructors of machinery, who have themselves contributed to its
advance, have expressed to me their opinion that if
the Calculating Engine itself had entirely failed, the
money expended by Government in the attempt to
make it, would be well repaid by the advancement it
had caused in the art of mechanical construction.

It is somewhat singular, that whilst I had anticipated the difficulties of construction, I had not
foreseen a far greater difficulty, which, however,
was surmounted by the invention of the Mechanical
Notation.

The state of the *Difference Engine* at the time

it was abandoned by the Government, was as follows: A considerable portion of it had been made; a part (about sixteen figures) was put together; and the drawings, the whole of which are now in the Museum of King's College at Somerset House, were far advanced. Upon this engine the Government expended about £17,000.

The drawings of the *Analytical Engine* have been made entirely at *my own cost:* I instituted a long series of experiments for the purpose of reducing the expense of its construction to limits which might be within the means I could myself afford to supply. I am now resigned to the necessity of abstaining from its construction, and feel indisposed even to finish the drawings of one of its many general plans. As a slight idea of the state of the drawings may be interesting to some of my readers, I shall refer to a few of the great divisions of the subject.

ARITHMETICAL ADDITION. — About a dozen plans of different mechanical movements have been drawn. The last is of the very simplest order.

CARRIAGE OF TENS.—A larger number of drawings have been made of modes of carrying tens. They form two classes, in one of which the carriage takes place successively; in the other it occurs simultaneously, as will be more fully explained at the end of this chapter.

MULTIPLYING BY TENS.—This is a very important

process, though not difficult to contrive. Three modes are drawn; the difficulties are chiefly those of construction, and the most recent experiments now enable me to use the simplest form.

DIGIT COUNTING APPARATUS.—It is necessary that the machine should count the digits of the numbers it multiplies and divides, and that it should combine these properly with the number of decimals used. This is by no means so easy as the former operation : two or three systems of contrivances have been drawn.

COUNTING APPARATUS.—This is an apparatus of a much more general order, for treating the indices of functions and for the determination of the repetitions and movements of the Jacquard cards, on which the Algebraic developments of functions depend. Two or three such mechanisms have been drawn.

SELECTORS.—The object of the system of contrivances thus named, is to choose in the operation of Arithmetical division the proper multiple to be subtracted; this is one of the most difficult parts of the engine, and several different plans have been drawn. The one at last adopted is, considering the object, tolerably simple. Although division is an inverse operation, it is possible to perform it entirely by mechanism without any tentative process.

REGISTERING APPARATUS.—This is necessary in division to record the quotient as it arises. It is simple, and different plans have been drawn.

ALGEBRAIC SIGNS.—The means of combining these are very simple, and have been drawn.

PASSAGE THROUGH ZERO AND INFINITY.—This is one of the most important parts of the Engine, since it may lead to a totally different action upon the formulæ employed. The mechanism is much simpler than might have been expected, and is drawn and fully explained by notations.

BARRELS AND DRUMS.—These are contrivances for grouping together certain mechanical actions often required; they are occasionally under the direction of the cards; sometimes they guide themselves, and sometimes their own guidance is interfered with by the Zero Apparatus.

GROUPINGS.—These are drawings of several of the contrivances before described, united together in various forms. Many drawings of them exist.

GENERAL PLANS. — Drawings of all the parts necessary for the Analytical Engine have been made in many forms. No less than thirty different general plans for connecting them together, have been devised and partially drawn; one or two are far advanced. No. 25 was lithographed at Paris in 1840. These have been superseded by simpler or more powerful combinations, and the last and most simple has only been sketched.

A large number of Mechanical Notations exist, showing the movements of these several parts, and also explaining the processes of arithmetic and

N 2

algebra to which they relate.   One amongst them, for the process of division, covers nearly thirty large folio sheets.

About twenty years after I had commenced the first Difference Engine, and after the greater part of these drawings had been completed, I found that almost every contrivance in it had been superseded by new and more simple mechanism, which the construction of the Analytical Engine had rendered necessary.   Under these circumstances I made drawings of an entirely new Difference Engine.   The drawings, both for the calculating and the printing parts, amounting in number to twenty-four, are completed.   They are accompanied by the necessary mechanical notations, and by an index of letters to the drawings ; so that although there is as yet no description in words, there is effectively such a description by signs, that this new Difference Engine might be constructed from them.

Amongst the difficulties which surrounded the idea of the construction of an Engine for developing Analytical formulæ, there were some which seemed insuperable if not impossible, not merely to the common understandings of well-informed persons, but even to the more practised intellect of some of the greatest masters of that science which the machine was intended to control.   It still seemed, after much discussion, at least highly doubtful whether such formulæ could ever be brought within the grasp of mechanism.

I have met in the course of my inquiries with four cases of obstacles presenting the appearance of impossibilities. As these form a very interesting chapter in the history of the human mind, and are on the one hand connected with some of the simplest elements of mechanism, and on the other with some of the highest principles of philosophy, I shall endeavour to explain them in a short, and, I hope, somewhat popular manner, to those who have a very moderate share of mathematical knowledge. Those of my readers to whom they may not be sufficiently interesting, will, I hope, excuse the interruption, and pass on to the succeeding chapters.

§ The first difficulty arose at an early stage of the Analytical Engine. The mechanism necessary to add one number to another, if the carriage of the tens be neglected, is very simple. Various modes had been devised and drawings of about a dozen contrivances for carrying the tens had been made. The same general principle pervaded all of them. Each figure wheel when receiving addition, in the act of passing from nine to ten caused a lever to be put aside. An axis with arms arranged spirally upon it then revolved, and commencing with the lowest figure replaced successively those levers which might have been put aside during the addition. This replacing action upon the levers caused unity to be added to the figure wheel next above. The numerical example below will illustrate the process.

597,999 ⎫
201,001 ⎬ Numbers to be added.

798,990   Sum without any carriage.
      1   Puts aside lever acting on tens.

798,900   First spiral arm adds tens and
      1   puts aside the next lever.

798,000   Second spiral arm adds hundreds, and
      1   puts aside the next lever.

799,000   Third spiral arm adds thousands.

Now there is in this mechanism a certain analogy with the act of memory. The lever thrust aside by the passage of the tens, is the equivalent of the note of an event made in the memory, whilst the spiral arm, acting at an after time upon the lever put aside, in some measure resembles the endeavours made to recollect a fact.

It will be observed that in these modes of *carrying*, the action must be *successive*. Supposing a number to consist of thirty places of figures, each of which is a nine, then if any other number of thirty figures be added to it, since the addition of each figure to the corresponding one takes place at the same time, the whole addition will only occupy nine units of time. But since the number added may be unity, the carriages may possibly amount to twenty-nine.   Consequently the time of making the carriages may be more than three times as long as that required for addition.

The time thus occupied was, it is true, very considerably shortened in the Difference Engine : but when the Analytical Engine was to be contrived, it became essentially necessary to diminish it still further.   After much time fruitlessly expended in many contrivances and drawings, a very different principle, which seemed indeed at first to be impossible, suggested itself.

It is evident that whenever a carriage is conveyed to the figure above, if that figure happen to be a nine, a new carriage must then take place. and so on as far as the nines extend.   Now the principle sought to be expressed in mechanism amounted to this.

1st. That a lever should be put aside, as before, on the passage of a figure-wheel from nine to ten.

2d. That the engine should then ascertain the position of all those nines which by carriage would ultimately become zero, and give notice of new carriages ; that, foreseeing those events, it should anticipate the result by making all the carriages simultaneously.

This was at last accomplished, and many different mechanical contrivances fulfilling these conditions were drawn.   The former part of this mechanism bears an analogy to memory, the latter to foresight.   The apparatus remembers as it were, one set of events, the transits from nine to ten : examines what nines are found in certain critical places : then, in consequence of the concurrence of these events, acts at once so as to anticipate other actions that would have happened at a more distant period, had less artificial means been used.

§ The second apparent impossibility seemed to present far greater difficulty. Fortunately it was not one of immediate *practical* importance, although as a question of philosophical inquiry it possessed the highest interest. I had frequently discussed with Mrs. Somerville and my highly gifted friend the late Professor M'Cullagh of Dublin, the question whether it was possible that we should be able to treat algebraic formulæ by means of machinery. The result of many inquiries led to the conclusion, that if not really impossible, it was almost hopeless. The first difficulty was that of representing an indefinite number in a machine of finite size. It was readily admitted that if a machine afforded means of operating on *all* numbers under twenty places of figures, then that any number, or *an indefinite* number, of less than twenty places or figures might be represented by it. But such number will not be really indefinite. It would be possible to make a machine capable of operating upon numbers of forty, sixty, or one hundred places of figures : still, however, a limit must at last be reached, and the numbers represented would not be really *indefinite*. After lengthened consideration of this subject, the solution of the difficulty was discovered; and it presented the appearance of reasoning in a circle.

Algebraical operations in their most general form cannot be carried on by machinery without the capability of expressing *indefinite* constants. On the other hand, the only way of arriving at the expression of an indefinite constant, was through the intervention of Algebra itself.

This is not a fit place to enter into the detail of the means employed, further than to observe, that it was found possible to evade the difficulty, by connecting *indefinite* number with the *infinite in time* instead of with the *infinite in space*.

The solution of this difficulty being found, and the discovery of another principle having been made, namely—that *the nature of a function might be indicated by its position*—algebra, in all its most abstract forms, was placed completely within the reach of mechanism.

§ The third difficulty that presented itself was one which I had long before anticipated. It was proposed to me nearly at the same time by three of the most eminent cultivators of analysis then existing, M. Jacobi, M. Bessel, and Professor M'Cullagh, who were examining the drawings of the Analytical Engine. The question they proposed was this :—How would the Analytical Engine be able to treat calculations in which the use of tables of logarithms, sines, &c. or any other tabular numbers should be required?

My reply was, that as at the time logarithms were invented, it became necessary to remodel the whole of the formulæ of Trigonometry, in order to adapt it to the new instrument of calculation: so when the Analytical Engine is made, it will be desirable to transform all formulæ containing tabular numbers into others better adapted to the use of such a machine. This, I replied, is the answer I give to you as mathematicians; but I added, that for others less skilled in our science, I had another answer: namely—

That the engine might be so arranged that where-ever tabular numbers of any kind, occurred in a formula given it to compute, it would on arriving at any required tabular number, as for instance, if it required the logarithm of 1207, stop itself, and ring a bell to call the attendant, who would find written at a certain part of the machine " Wanted log. of 1207." The attendant would then fetch from tables previously computed by the engine, the logarithm it required, and placing it in the proper place, would lift a detent, permitting the engine to continue its work.

The next step of the engine, on receiving the tabular number (in this case the logarithm of 1207) would be to *verify* the fact of its being really that logarithm. In case no mistake had been made by the attendant, the engine would use the given tabular number, and go on with its work until some other tabular number were required, when the same process would be repeated. If, however, any mistake had been made by the attendant, and a wrong logarithm had been accidentally given to the engine, it would have discovered the mistake, and have rung a louder bell to call the attention of its guide, who on looking at the proper place, would see a plate above the logarithm he had just put in with the word "*wrong*" engraven upon it.

By such means it would be perfectly possible to make all calculations requiring tabular numbers, without the chance of error.

Although such a plan does not seem absolutely impossible, it has always excited, in those informed of it for the first time, the greatest surprise. How, it has been often asked, does it happen if the engine knows when the *wrong* logarithm is offered to it, that it does not also know the right one; and if so, what is the necessity of having recourse to the attendant to supply it? The solution of this difficulty is accomplished by the very simplest means.

§ The fourth of the apparent impossibilities to which I have referred, involves a condition of so extraordinary a nature that even the most fastidious inquirer into the powers of the Analytical Engine could scarcely require it to fulfil.

Knowing the kind of objections that my countrymen make to this invention, I proposed to myself this inquiry :—

Is it possible so to construct the Analytical Engine, that after the cards representing the formulæ and numbers are put into it, and the handle is turned, the following condition shall be fulfilled?

The attendant shall stop the machine in the middle of its work, whenever he chooses, and as often as he pleases. At each stoppage he shall examine all the figure wheels, and if he can, without breaking the machine, move any of them to other figures, he shall be at liberty to do so. Thus he may from time to time, falsify as many numbers as he pleases. Yet notwithstanding this, the final calculation and all the intermediate steps shall be entirely free from error. I have succeeded in fulfilling this condition by means of a principle in itself very simple. It may add somewhat, though not very much, to the amount of mechanism required; in many parts of the engine the principle has been already carried out. I by no means think such a plan *necessary*, although wherever it can be accomplished without expense it ought to be adopted.

CHAPTER XIV.

SCIENCE in England is not a profession : its cultivators are scarcely recognised even as a class. Our language itself contains no *single* term by which their occupation can be expressed. We borrow a foreign word [*Savant*] from another country whose high ambition it is to advance science, and whose deeper policy, in accord with more generous feelings, gives to the intellectual labourer reward and honour, in return for services which crown the nation with imperishable renown, and ultimately enrich the human race.

The first question which presents itself to a government desirous of advancing science, is to consider what departments of knowledge it is important that it should reward. This is a point upon which much misunderstanding prevails, and with regard to which interested parties have studiously endeavoured to delude the public.

As the fund which can be applied to this purpose even by a generous nation, is moderate, the first limitation of its application ought naturally to be,—to confine it to those discoveries which are from their very nature not immediately capable of becoming a source of profit.

One of the most common errors, is to reward persons who have merely acquired an extensive knowledge of various departments of science, but who have neither extended its boundaries by new methods, nor added new principles to its theories.

§ An analogous mistake often occurs to wealthy and benevolent persons residing in the country, who, finding in the son of their village blacksmith or other artificer, some great aptitude for figures, immediately conclude that if properly trained and then sent to College, he will turn out a great mathematician. Now although in very rare instances such cases may have occurred, the general result is quite different. The lad thus selected, if as is usually the case he is somewhat above the average intellect, will under such favourable circumstances probably acquire a considerable knowledge of science, and become a very respectable member of society. But if the benevolent person who thus totally changed the position in life of this young man, had first made inquiries at our national schools, he would probably have found several out of every hundred scholars, capable under similar treatment of acquiring a still larger amount of that knowledge.

§ With the increasing extension of science the labour of some of its details becomes excessive, and those who are able to afford the expense, gladly employ computers to relieve them from the more irksome portions of their toil. The reduction of astronomical and meteorological observations are of this kind. When once the formulæ to be used are decided upon, and a skeleton form is ruled or printed and a system of checks is devised, the remaining work may be executed by persons of very moderate attainments. This may be extended to the computation of the orbits of planets, of comets, and of double stars, and such assistance may usually be had on very moderate terms. In more extensive operations, the liability to error from the want of sufficient checks, and the great tediousness and even uncertainty of the result must remain, until mechanism shall entirely relieve the mind from these difficulties.

§ Let us now consider what is the present situation of men of science in England.

The estimate which is formed of the social position of any class of society, depends mainly upon the answer to these two questions :—

What are the salaries of the highest offices to which the most successful may aspire?

What are the honorary distinctions which the most eminent can attain?

Offices of a strictly scientific nature are few, and

their salaries are generally of small amount: amongst these there are—

A few of the professorships at our universities.

The Astronomer Royal.

The Astronomers of some of our Colonial Observatories.

The Master of Mechanics to the Queen.

The Conductor of the Nautical Almanac.

The Director of the Museum of Economical Geology and of the Geological Survey.

Various officers of the same institution.

Some of the officers in the Natural History department of the British Museum.

The most valuable of these, that of Astronomer Royal, receives about 1,300*l.* a-year, including a pension of 300*l.*

Thus there is amongst this class one solitary prize of at the utmost 1,300*l.* a-year, and that is confined to one department of science.

Offices for which men of science are at least as fit as any other persons, are numerous, though they are very rarely attained by those who pursue it.

It may, perhaps, have been expected that the recent appointment of Sir John Herschel to the Mastership of the Mint, should have been noticed in the previous list. But until the motives which dictated it are known, I have no observation to make, except that it is gratifying to me to find that the great principle of the "claims of science," for which I have all my life been contending, has been thus as it were, unconsciously admitted by the minister: and had the accident of birth placed me in his position, the appointment would have been the same, although the motives for it might have been different.

Let us now turn to the *honorary distinctions* which await science. During the eleven years of the present reign, one solitary instance is to be found of a baronetcy given for science, and that too occurred only at a festival (the coronation) at which baronetages and peerages were showered upon those whose sole claim was founded on the mere support of party.

During the same interval, about half a dozen of those who cultivate science, have been knighted.

It appears then that the highest position a man of science can attain, and that but very rarely, is a baronetcy; that the highest salary is about 1,000*l.* a-year. When this is compared with the most successful prizes in the army, the navy, the church, or the bar, it shows at once the inferior position occupied by science.

Connected with the navy is an office which ought to be held by a person eminently uniting science with practical skill. The Surveyor-General of the Navy has to decide upon questions of the greatest difficulty. The mathematical theories and inquiries on which the various qualities of sailing vessels and steamers depend, are of the most complicated kind, and are not even yet sufficiently advanced to serve as secure and absolute guides. Yet without a know-- ledge of their present state, and a power of advancing those theories, it is hopeless to expect the greatest and most valuable additions to the science of naval architecture. This can only be accomplished by one who combines a great facility in applying such portions of them as admit of it, to the practical facts which experience is continually bringing to light.

The talent for commanding a fleet is by no means rare : the most successful in that line may attain fortune, the peerage, and a large pension. The talent for investigating the laws regulating the forms of ships, is of the very rarest order. Even if its possessor should happen to be of the naval profession, his greatest reward could only extend to knighthood, and a thousand a-year during the tenure of an office of great labour. Of course, naval men having the requisite talents, would never turn them into so unprofitable a direction : yet it would be difficult to say how many millions of money have been, and continue to be, uselessly expended for want of that knowledge.

Amongst those situations in the appointment of the government, there are many in which a knowledge of various branches of science is highly useful. A considerable number of these are filled by officers of engineers, artillery, and other corps of the army and of the navy. Thus those whose service is already paid for by the country, are excused from doing their ordinary duty, and are paid again for doing another and perhaps a more agreeable duty.

Under the delusive plea that *military* and *civil* engineering are the same science, military engineers have been placed in situations for which they were unfit, and civil engineers have been excluded, to the injury of that profession, and to the much greater damage of the country. The Ordnance Magnetical Observatories will furnish an example of the *economy* which, it is pretended, results from such arrangements.

Some ten or twelve years ago, it was proposed by Humboldt that various governments should establish magnetical observatories at different points on the earth's surface, so chosen that by the united information thus obtained, we might arrive at more accurate and correct ideas of the state of the earth's magnetism. That plan has been pursued with great advantage to science. A magnetical observatory was built at Greenwich, and continuous observations were made which have been reduced and published annually under the direction of the Astronomer Royal. The expense* of the Magnetic and Meteoric Observatory, excluding that portion of the Astronomer Royal's salary which may be

* See App. to Rept. of Select Com. on Misc. Expenditure, p. 222.

considered due to his services in the direction of this department, but *including the whole of the making and recording the observations themselves,* is 720*l.* annually.

There are other magnetical observatories in several of our colonies in which observations are made. These observations appear to be sent for reduction to an establishment at Woolwich, under the superintendence of Colonel Sabine.

Now the first and most obvious course would have been to have employed an additional number of computers at Greenwich, who should use the same formulæ and methods of reduction. This would ensure perfect uniformity, and would apparently be the most economical plan.

The course that is actually pursued is to have a separate establishment at Woolwich, with an officer, and several non-commissioned officers on extra pay, so that the account stands thus :—*

	£	s.	d.
One officer, extra pay	182	10	0
One non-commissioned officer, ditto . .	27	7	6
Three non-commissioned officers, ditto .	68	8	9
Contingent, not exceeding . . .	200	0	0
Apparent expense .	£478	6	3

But to this must be added—

	£	s.	d.
The full pay of Lieut.-Colonel . .	300	0	5
His extra pay	273	15	0
Carried forward .	£1,052	1	8

* See p. 221 App. to Rept. on Misc. Expenditure, p. 848 (543) II.

	£	s.	d.
Brought forward .	1,052	1	8
Full pay of one officer, if a Captain . .	192	16	3
Ditto one non-commissioned ditto* . .	20	0	0
Ditto three ditto ditto	50	0	0
Real expense .	£1,314	17	11

In the estimate for civil service for 1850† the following items occur :—

	£	s.	d.
Extra pay to Colonel Sabine, Royal Artillery, for services in connexion with the Magnetic and Meteorological Observations, for ten years, from 7th May, 1839, to 7th May, 1849, at 15s. a-day	2,739	15	0
Deduct 3s. 4d. per day granted him from 1st June, 1841, to 7th May, 1848, as compensation for loss of command pay . . .	434	8	0
	£2,305	7	0

This certainly requires an explanation. Here is an officer not doing the services of his profession, who it seems has been allowed a compensation for what he *might* have received if he *had* rendered those services : notwithstanding which, at the end of ten years, he claims and is allowed the above sum of £2,305 7s. for services the payment of which it would seem by this account was never contemplated during those ten years.

* The pay of the non-commissioned officers has been assumed as somewhat less by ten per cent. than their extra pay.

† See p. 41, App. to Rept. on Misc. Expenditure, p. 848, (268) IV.

It is also to be remarked that Colonel Sabine does not reside at Woolwich, where the only effective portion of the work is carried on.

§ But to return to our argument : it is singular that even the principles on which science ought to be rewarded, are not entirely settled.

Should all equally great discoveries be rewarded in the same way, without regard to the different positions in society which the discoverers occupy ? If this principle were admitted, the rewards must be very large, or there would be none for the higher classes of society.

Of all steps in the social scale, that which first elevates a man into the class of Gentlemen is by far the greatest. In this country, where the differences of rank are great, there is fortunately, until we approach royalty, no absolute line of demarcation between any classes, except the one alluded to ; even the peerage to a private gentleman is not so great an advance.

It is without doubt very desirable that all classes should contribute to the intellectual advancement of the country. But unless different advantages are proposed to different classes, it is not possible to apply any general stimulus to all.

§ Those who maintain that science is its own reward, cannot have remarked the vicious circle in which they reason. The delight derived from discovery is indeed a high intellectual reward, but the force of this maxim is only known practically to those who have already advanced in the career of discovery : it can, therefore, never direct the inquirer into that line.   All men are subject to the same feelings and passions.   It is assuredly true that men of wealth and rank will be happier if they cultivate their faculties, and add to the amount of human knowledge : but they cannot be aware of this truth until they are considerably advanced, consequently it cannot have induced them to commence this cultivation.

§ But it is for the interest of those who are the consumers of knowledge, that all other minds should be induced to advance it : therefore it is our interest to place even before the highest classes, at the commencement of their career, motives for its pursuit.   Having raised such expectations, justice requires us to fulfil them ; nor can we regret that the advantages derived from the course into which we have invited them, should have proved beneficial to them beyond even the limits of our prediction.

It is of the very nature of knowledge that the recondite and apparently useless acquisition of to-day, becomes part of the popular food of a succeeding generation.   Thus the nobleman who spends his wealth in constructing unrivalled instruments, and his nights in scrutinizing with them the remotest boundaries of space into which human vision has yet penetrated, is preparing a source of pleasure and happiness for the descendants of those very peasants whom his practical skill in engineering has raised by his own instructions above the ranks in which he originally found them.

§ Another question has been raised, but not yet answered, respecting those pensions which have been awarded for scientific discoveries. A certain definite limit has been fixed by practice, which has never yet been exceeded in pensions assigned to science. The sum of three hundred a-year, the maximum of reward to science, is almost the minimum of reward for other services.

The most important question is, Whether these pensions are given as the reward of scientific services rendered to the country, or as charity to enlightened and studious persons who happen to be poor? In the one case, they are an honour which a philosopher may be proud of receiving from his country: in the other, they are no more than a higher order of pauper relief, which an independent gentleman can scarcely condescend to accept.

Another important question, though of a different nature, also arises here. Are these pensions, thus small in amount, fit to be offered to those who, in order to arrive at their discoveries, have themselves in some cases spent out of their own private fortune, sums far larger than the fee simple of the rewards thus offered to them.

Is it just that the *same rewards* should be given to persons filling well-endowed scientific offices, supplied with all the means of discovery which the most perfect art can produce, as to other philosophers, who, at the expense of their own personal comfort and perhaps of the interests of their family, have purchased the costly means by which they have succeeded in *equally* improving their several departments of science?

For the honour and the advancement of science, it is necessary that these questions should be distinctly answered. It is to be hoped that some independent member of parliament will at last press them in a manner which no ministerial shuffling can evade.

CHAPTER XV.

THE PRESS.

SOME of the principles for the discovery of truth, professed and acted upon by those who administer the laws of England, and by those who practice in its courts, are certainly repugnant to the first impressions and feelings of honest men, if not also to common sense. It is, therefore, absolutely necessary, in order to remove these impressions, to state the ground on which those principles are defended. That ground may be shortly expressed thus—

It has been found by long experience that it is more for the advantage of truth and justice that professional men should be stimulated by fees and the hope of advancement, to put forward or conceal every fact, to advance, withhold, or oppose every inference and argument, *solely* as it may be of advantage to the party by whom they are employed.

It is also stated that the public are aware of this convention, and, therefore, are not deceived by the speeches of the advocate.

Without asking whether the long experience alluded to has ever been fortified by the trial and the failure of an opposite course, it may be at once stated that this mode of arriving at truth is contrary to the result of long experience in matters of science. In all discussions on those subjects, it is found far more conducive to truth, if either party in discussing a mooted point discover in his own argument a flaw, unobserved by his opponent, that he should immediately point it out, and that they should both apply their minds to repair it, and if unsuccessful, admit it. The same course is pursued with regard to facts; every circumstance, however apparently remote, is contributed by both inquirers to the common stock, without the slightest care as to its bearings on one or the other side of the question. Facts thus conveyed for the first time to the mind of one of the parties, often recall to his memory analogous facts, and thus the materials of reasoning or of induction become largely increased.

§ To this supposed legal principle, it may be fairly objected that it is entirely a theoretical view. To be convinced of this it is enough to appeal to every man who has ever sat on a jury or heard one addressed by counsel. He well knows that the very first effort of the learned advocate is to attempt to persuade the jury that he is no advocate at all. This line is sustained throughout his address, and

his great object is to convince them that he himself personally believes both the facts to which his
witnesses testify, and the inferences he adduces
from their evidence.   The more skilful the advocate,
the more he endeavours to persuade the jury that
he is merely an impartial observer, assisting them
in arriving at a just conclusion.

The effects of long habit in thus mystifying less
practised reasoners, cannot fail to be injurious to
the moral character of the man.   Take a case of
title to property, on which a barrister is consulted.
Suppose the holder has no right whatever to it, yet
will the barrister by every means his knowledge
and ingenuity can suggest, help his client to rob
some other person of his property.   It is useless to
say that in such circumstances the attorney con-
ceals certain facts of his case, and does not put the
facts to the counsel in this plain way.   On such
occasions the most skilful counsel are always employed, and they are certainly competent, *if they
choose it*, to ascertain the real state of the case.   In
criminal cases such attempts to mislead juries are
still more reprehensible.

§ If the principle now discussed is sound, it
is capable of application to another subject—the
press.   But strangely enough, lawyers, more than
any other class, abuse the press because it treats
its subject commercially, and refuse to admit that
rule in the case of editors of newspapers, which

they claim as a sanction for themselves. A little examination, however, will show that the conduct of the press is much more defensible than that of the bar.

The public require a daily account of all facts connected with politics and the institutions of the country; it also demands analyses, discussions, and opinions on the bearings of all such facts upon its interests. As opinions amongst the public are often much opposed to, or widely different from each other, it is clear that this demand cannot be satisfied without many newspapers. Now, looking solely to the commercial profit arising from its sale, it is tolerably certain that some one paper supported by greater capital, and conducted with greater skill, will endeavour to represent the opinions of the largest class of those who purchase these sheets of diurnal information. The first place being thus occupied, other journals will arise to represent the opinions of smaller, yet, perhaps, of powerful classes. Thus the opinions of all parties, and, in some measure, their relative strength, become known to each other. This is an end much to be desired.

If the opinions of the public change, those of the leading journal must of course follow, even though they are directly opposed to those advocated by it a few days before. Such a change undoubtedly shocks the feelings of many who remain constant to their own views, and cases often occur in which these latter give up their usual paper. It must, however, be admitted that there are few political or economical questions on which one side is morally right, the other morally wrong. That a given man has or has not got possession of another man's estate, that a man has or has not committed a murder or other crime, must, in most cases, be well known to his counsel; if in either case the wrong-doer escapes punishment, an injury is done to society. But whether a given line of policy or a given law, is more or less beneficial or even injurious to the State, is generally dependent on so many causes that very few are able to foresee their consequences with tolerable certainty.

The most general and unsophisticated opinion is, that no man is justified in advocating, even when unpaid, doctrines in which he does not himself believe. With respect to the press, it is possible that the writer of the second article may be a different individual from the person who wrote the first article; but even were he the same person, the bar at least have no right to find fault with him.

§ The press then may advantageously be considered as expressing the opinions of classes, not of individuals. It has greatly improved in the last quarter of a century, in consequence of the general improvement of all classes.

There is now also fortunately established a certain

professional feeling amongst its members that reports of speeches, or of facts, ought to be *rigidly exact*. Abstracts of speeches will occasionally be coloured not by additions, but by selections or omissions, according to the side of the question advocated by the writer. Yet even here the more popular papers are careful to do justice to all parties. It is the more important that this latter rule should be admitted as a principle, because, from the great length of the debates themselves, they are rarely read by persons much occupied, except when questions of great interest occur.

To such persons an *impartial* abstract is invaluable.

In the leading articles greater latitude is allowable. These, if the theory which has been explained is admitted, are avowedly the expressions of the opinion of its customers. The power of the press is undoubtedly great, yet it is bound by the strongest ties of interest not to abuse that power. It is clearly its interest to seem consistent, and consequently to employ, at almost any expense, the best means of ascertaining the opinions of the country *before* they are publicly expressed. Having attained this knowledge, it will get the credit of appearing to lead public opinion.

Its powers of doing good when honestly conducted, are yet larger than its powers of mischief. Yet even here its power is of necessity limited. It cannot advocate even the *best* course of policy on any important subject unless it is tolerably certain that it will succeed in convincing its customers that it is *really* the best. It *ought* not to advocate that best course, because the falling off of its subscribers might then disable it from as effectually assisting the *second best*. It, however, neither ought, nor is it ultimately its interest, to conceal those opinions from its subscribers.

The power it possesses, of exposing knaves and swindlers, by means of its correspondents, and of sending highly intelligent commissioners from time to time to inquire personally into the situation of various classes of the population, are of great value, and could only be exercised by a wealthy as well as by a powerful press.

CHAPTER XVI.

PARTY.

"Of all the tyrannies that molest this terrestrial scene perhaps there is none so arbitrary, so extravagant, or so grotesque as the tyranny of party. There is none that so frequently subjects the wise to the caprices of the fool, and the good to the designs of the knave."—*The Times, Dec.* 1850.

THERE are two great principles of government which divide the opinions of mankind.

1st. Unchangeableness; or, "Let things alone :"—the law of the Medes and Persians.

2d. Progress; or, the continual advancement of mankind in the improvement of their Institutions.

No number of persons sufficiently extensive to deserve the name of a class, have ever advocated the principle of *Retrocession*. Some few enthusiasts have indeed believed in a golden age, and have advocated the pastoral, or even the hunting life. These, however, were not persons capable of collecting, examining, and weighing the evidence on which alone an opinion on the comparative happiness of people existing in a savage or in a civilized state of life can justly be formed.

P

A larger number exist, the admirers of the past, each perhaps the worshipper of his own peculiar age. Had he lived in those times, enjoying only the ordinary capacity he now possesses, but endowed with all the increased knowledge of the present day, he might then have attained a position more commensurate with his wishes, though quite disproportioned to the industry of his exertions or the calibre of his intellect.

§ In our own country, "the wisdom of our ancestors" is with some the hackneyed theme of unbounded admiration.

Our ancestors were generally wise and sagacious men : they applied their energies and their knowledge, as far as it went, to their *existing* wants and necessities. Those amongst them who deserved that character, would, if questioned, have expressed in language the precept to which their deeds conformed. Availing themselves gratefully of all the knowledge bequeathed to them by their predecessors, they struggled to advance it for their own and their children's benefit, and thus they might have counselled every generation to their latest posterity :—

"You have received from us, tested by many trials, " the treasured knowledge, gathered under difficulty " and danger, of our country's experience."

" Let the great object of each generation be to " purify that body of knowledge from its partial

" errors, to add to it the greatest amount of new
" truths.

" Remember that accumulated knowledge, like
" accumulated capital, increases at compound inte-
" rest: but it differs from the accumulation of
" capital in this; that the increase of knowledge
" produces a more rapid rate of progress, whilst the
" accumulation of capital leads to a lower rate of
" interest. Capital thus checks its own accumula-
" tion: knowledge thus accelerates it own advance.
" Each generation, therefore, to deserve comparison
" with its predecessor, is bound to add much more
" largely to the common stock than that which it
" immediately succeeds."

§ A question has not unfrequently been proposed
by those who apply their foresight to remote rather
than to immediate objects—

" What will become of our posterity when our
" coal-fields are exhausted?"

The best answer to this question is, that when
that distant day arrives, if our posterity, with the
accumulated knowledge of centuries, shall have
failed to find any substitute for coal in the many
other sources of heat which nature supplies, they
will then deserve to be frost-bitten.

§ It is remarkable that the great parties adopt
opposite principles in pursuance of the same line of
reasoning.

The advocates of things as they are, wish to stop

all change, in order to *prevent revolution.* Those who inculcate continual progress, support it, because it makes all changes gradual, and thus, in their opinion, it *prevents revolution.*

It is by sudden changes in laws and institutions that the greatest misery is inflicted on mankind. Those gradual changes which are spread over a considerable period are foreseen, and men make preparation beforehand to accommodate themselves to the new but expected circumstances.

If the changes effected by the Reform Bill, had been spread over the ten preceding and ten subsequent years, few will deny that it would have been a better measure, and more effective for its purpose. The experience derived from its earlier changes would then have been available for its later uses. The pertinacity, however, with which all reform was resisted, led to such a state of affairs, that after the refusal to transfer the franchise from East Retford, revolution was averted only by vast and *immediate* concession.

§ The terms Tory and Whig had been the watchwords of these two parties, until, at last, the public lost all confidence in either. With the increasing wealth of the country, and with the greater application of observation, of reasoning, and of science, to its many arts and manufactures, a vast increase has been produced in the numbers, the power, and the influence of the middle classes. Many individuals who have raised themselves by their intellect and industry into this class, have been so fully impressed with the advantages of previous training, that they have made efforts to give their children an education more extensive and more liberal than any which, until lately, our universities had attempted to supply.

It is to the growth of this class, which includes men possessing from 500*l.* to 5,000*l.* a-year, that we are indebted for much of the strength which public opinion now exerts upon the ministry of the day. Notwithstanding the vast influence of wealth and of rank throughout the country, there are still amongst these middle classes, thousands whose moderation renders them rich; who, therefore, can afford to be honest, and whose approbation is neither to be purchased by wealth, nor won by the seductions of rank and of fashionable life.

Such men, on all public questions, influence widely and justly the opinions of those around them. There are such in the House of Commons; and, with the extension of knowledge, many more will be added to their number.

Thus the very weakness of an administration may possibly become an advantage, since it thus becomes impossible for government to carry any measure entirely opposed to the calm good sense of the people. This, however, admits of one excepted case. If a party to advance its own interests will pander to some strong passion, to some prejudice of ignorance or of bigotry, it may for a time succeed, though it will ultimately lose in character.

In the meantime, the people have found out that Party is made use of only for the aggrandizement of a few families; that it has degenerated into a clique, banded together for mercenary purposes, without enthusiasm or genius to compensate for its meanness, and with little of talent to palliate its want of integrity.

The reign of party, however, verges towards its end; the supplies on which it feeds are sapped by economical reform. That almost all places under Government are greatly overpaid admits of no denial. The demand for them is notoriously great, and it is equally notorious that nothing but the strongest political interest has any chance in the contest for them.

The government of England is nominally a limited monarchy, but practically almost an oligarchy. A large number of its appointments are shared by a few families, into which some daring and unscrupulous intruders occasionally force their way, by opposition which it is easier to quell by place than to answer by argument : or into which less gifted and more cunning supporters sometimes obtain an entrance by a judicious alliance.

§ It is strongly asserted that government cannot go on without party. That those who maintain this opinion are incapable of so conducting it, must be at once admitted.

Without, however, entering into the debateable question of the *limits* of party, it is sufficient to state another principle, which no honest man will deny, and then to leave to the advocates of party to reconcile it with their doctrine.

It is morally wrong to endeavour to convince any one of the truth of an opinion in which the advocate himself does not believe.

If this principle were practically acted upon, how much of the valuable time of both Houses of Parliament would be saved! In looking over a debate, or still better, a *division,* the private opinions of many of the speakers are often well known by their friends to be quite at variance with the doctrines they advocated in their speeches. The quasi-honesty of those who admit the truth in private, is however venial, when compared with the hypocrisy of those who are equally false on both occasions.

Party, then, as it practically exists, is one of the evils of the political state of England.

The remedy must come partly from the reduction of temptation, by diminishing the salaries of all those places and appointments for which there is such immense competition; partly from the effect of public opinion; and ultimately, to a far greater extent, when any sincere desire exists to restrain it, from improved methods of distributing patronage.

But one defect seems almost always to accompany a high state of civilization, namely,—a great deficiency of moral courage in large classes of persons, who from knowledge and position ought rightly to contribute their share to the formation and expression of public opinion. The first evil which this produces, is an excessive zeal and energy in a few of those who are most strongly convinced. These bear the brunt of the attacks of all who are interested in the support of abuses. If, unhappily, they are not independent in fortune as well as in spirit, these, the forlorn hope of reform, are sure ultimately to be trampled upon and destroyed by the jobbers—they die with ruined fortunes and broken hearts.

Many of those who shared their opinions, and urged on their enthusiasm, but who warily abstained from expressing their own thoughts *in public*, now venture to avow those principles, to which opinion has at length advanced: these reap the rewards won by the energies and sacrifices of their martyred friends. For such, the epithet the poet applied to Bacon is not unfit:

—" the wisest—meanest of mankind."—Pope.

A very serious evil arises from this timidity in expressing opinions. The whole state of society presents a counterfeit surface,—no man knows how many or how few really share his opinions: its whole fabric is in a state of unstable equilibrium;

it is liable at every moment to most unlooked-for changes, from accidents apparently trivial.

The following is one amongst many examples which might have been selected of the different standard with which Party measures services rendered to the public by those within and those without its own limits.

In the year 1847, when some millions of English money were sent over to save the people of Ireland from perishing by famine, it became necessary to organize a system of accounts and of regulations, for the direction of those officers who were sent over for the purpose of personally superintending the distribution of this relief.

These arrangements were made by the Assistant Secretary of the Treasury, Sir C. T——, K.C.B., at extra hours; but it does not appear how many months he was so employed.

The office at that time held by this gentleman, was one for which he received a salary of £2,500 per annum; and certainly this liberal salary ought to have commanded the devotion of his whole time, if necessary, to the public service. It would seem that some application was made from the Treasury, and that Lord John Russell acceded to it with unwonted liberality. He gave the remuneration in a manner thought unconstitutional by several eminent members of the House of Commons, and to an extent justly considered extravagant by the public.

The following extracts from Hansard will explain
the matter.

"The Chancellor of the Exchequer.—With regard to Sir
C. T——, the case was an exceptional one ; but his services on
the extraordinary emergency alluded to were so very great
that it had been thought right to make a Treasury minute,
awarding him £2,500. The item would be found in the
' Civil Contingencies ' laid before the House.

"Mr. Disraeli,—while readily acknowledging the great
services rendered by this gentleman, could not forget that the
Order of the Bath had been conferred upon him—a reward
bestowed upon him as for services which could not be paid by a
pecuniary grant. The vote of £2,500 was surely conceived in
rather bad taste ; and a *preux chevalier* like Sir C. T——,
bearing his blushing honours, might well be supposed to recoil
from receiving an extra year's salary.

" Mr. Gladstone—condemned the conduct of Government
in this matter. It was their duty to have submitted a vote
to the House, not to have taken on themselves to reward a
public servant. If there was one rule connected with the
public service which more than any other ought to be scrupu-
lously observed, it was this, that the salary of a public officer,
more especially if he were of high rank, ought to cover all
the services he might be called upon to render. Any departure from this rule must be dangerous.

" Lord John Russell said, that the Government thought the
services of Sir C. T—— were deserving of reward.

"Mr. Goulburn.—According to all precedent, the House of
Commons ought to have fixed the amount of Sir C. T.'s remuneration.

" Lord John Russell.—Sir C. T—— stated in his evidence
that he worked three hours before breakfast; that he then went
to the Treasury, where he worked all day ; and that the pressure upon him was such that he wondered that he had been
able to get through it alive."—*Hansard*, Vol. 101, p. 138,
1848. Supply, 14th Aug. 1848.

There appears to be some indistinctness as to the fund out of which this 2,500*l.* was taken. Compare Hansard with Questions 1693 and 1696 of the Report on Miscellaneous Expenditure.

No mode of keeping accounts, however, will alter the fact; that if the famine had not occurred, neither would the 2,500*l.* have been required; consequently, that sum was part of the whole amount our humanity cost us.

The liberality of the Minister to the Assistant Secretary of the Treasury, may be explained by stating that he was the *brother-in-law* of a Cabinet Minister.

There was another gentleman at least equal in talent to the Assistant Secretary, whose services were gratuitous, who, at the risk of his health, was actively engaged on the spot in superintending the distribution of the relief. To him the Government thought it sufficient to give the Companionship of the Bath, whilst the Assistant Secretary was made a Commander of that Order.

CHAPTER XVII.

REWARDS OF MERIT.

THE personal distinctions in the gift of the Government of this country consist of the following five orders of knighthood :—

NAME.	NO. OF MEMBERS.		
	GRAND CROSS.	KNIGHT COM.	COMP.
The Garter - - -	25		
The Thistle - - -	16		
St. Patrick - - -	16		
The Bath { Military - -	50	102	525
{ Civil - -	25	50	200
St. George and St Michael -	15	20	25
	147	172	750

Of these, the first three are restricted, with few and rare exceptions, to persons of a certain rank—including earls, and those above them. The number of these, with the addition of three sons for each duke, and of the eldest sons of marquesses, amounts to about four hundred and fifty. Amongst this favoured class fifty-seven ribbons may be conferred; so that about one-eighth of the class enjoy the decoration.

These ribbons, although much sought after by the class amongst which they are distributed, are more correctly appreciated by the public at large.

With some illustrious and honourable exceptions, they are usually given by those in power to their party supporters. They have also occasionally been employed by the minister of the day, as inducements to persuade his friends to postpone inconvenient questions, to the agitation of which they had been publicly pledged.

An amusing and characteristic anecdote respecting one of these Orders, the Garter, is related of a late Premier. At a time when several of these " baubles" had fallen vacant, and been judiciously given away by the discreet minister, a friend asked him, why he had not retained a Garter for himself? to which he wittily replied, " Why, the fact is, I " don't see the use of a man's bribing himself."

The order of St. Michael and St. George was instituted for the Ionian Islands, and is usually given, after a certain time of service, to the Lord High Commissioner, to the Commanders-in-Chief of the Mediterranean fleet, and to other persons connected with the public service in those quarters.

Thus England has, practically, only one order of merit; and, singularly enough, with the exception of a few civil crosses of the first-class almost invariably given for diplomatic service, until lately,

that order was not accessible to any other than
military merit.

§ In countries, however, which we fondly flattered
ourselves were less advanced in civilization than our
own, the vulgar notion of paying homage to brute
force has long been superseded by a more just
appreciation of the elements of military glory.
Nations even the most ambitious of this species of
renown, have admitted that physical prowess, that
recklessness of personal danger, form but the smallest
amongst those qualities which contribute to military
success.

It is now felt and admitted, that it is the civil
capacity of the great commander which prepares the
way for his military triumphs; that his knowledge
of human nature enables him to select the fittest
agents, and to place them in the situations best
adapted to their powers; that his intimate acquaintance with all the accessaries which contribute to the
health and comfort of his troops, enables him to
sustain their moral and physical energy. It has
been seen that he must have studied and properly
estimated the character of his foes as well as of his
allies, and have made himself acquainted with the
personal character of the chiefs of both; and still further, that he must have scrutinized the secret motives which regulated their respective governments.

When directly engaged in the operations of contending armies occupying a wide extent of country,

he must be able, with rapid glance, to ascertain the force it is possible to concentrate upon each of many points in any given time, and the greater or less chance of failing in the attempt. He **must also** be able to foresee, with something more than conjecture, what amount of the enemy's force can be brought to the same spot in the same and in different times. With these elements he must undertake one of the most difficult of mental tasks, that of classifying and grouping the innumerable combinations to which either party may have recourse for purposes of attack or defence. Out of the multitude of such combinations, which might baffle by their simple enumeration the strongest memory, throwing aside the less important, he must be able to discover, to fix his attention, and to act upon the most favourable. Finally, when the course thus selected having been pursued, and perhaps partially carried out, is found to be entirely deranged by one of those many chances inseparable from such operations, then, in the midst of action, he must be able suddenly to organise a different system of operations, new to all other minds, yet possibly although unconsciously, anticipated by his own.

The genius that can meet and overcome such difficulties *must* be intellectual, and would, under different circumstances, have been distinguished in many a different career.

Nor even would it be very surprising that such a commander, estimating justly the extent of his own powers, and conscious of having planned the best combinations of which his mind is capable, should, having issued his orders, calmly lie down on the eve of the approaching conflict, and find in sleep that bodily restoration so indispensable to the full exercise of his faculties in the mighty struggle about to ensue.

§ It is not uninteresting to observe in society the opinions of its different classes respecting honours conferred on science. Military and naval men, especially the most eminent, feel that genius is limited by no profession, and themselves sympathizing with it, would gladly hail as brothers in the same distinction, the philosopher and the poet. With lawyers the case is reversed; genius dwells not in their courts : industry and acuteness, monopolised by one absorbing professional subject, exclude larger views ; and ribbons not being amongst the honoraria of their own profession, they reprobate their application to science. To this there are, however, some noble exceptions. Amongst the brightest ornaments of their own profession, men are to be found of larger experience and more extended views than it often produces, who are themselves qualified to have become discoverers in other sciences. It is much to be regretted when such powers are applied to the mere administration, instead of to the reformation, of the laws of their country.

It is difficult to pronounce on the opinion of the ministers of our Church as a body: one portion of them, by far the least informed, protests against anything which can advance the honour and the interests of science, because, in their limited and mistaken view, science is adverse to religion. This is not the place to argue that great question. It is sufficient to remark, that the best-informed and most enlightened men of all creeds and pursuits, agree that truth can never damage truth, and that every truth is allied indissolubly by chains more or less circuitous with all other truths; whilst error, at every step we make in its diffusion, becomes not only wider apart and more discordant from all truths, but has also the additional chance of destruction from all rival errors.

All established religions are, and must be in practice, political engines—they have all a strong tendency to self-aggrandisement. Our own is by no means exempt from this very natural infirmity.

The Church has been reproached with endeavouring to appropriate to itself all those professorships in our Universities which are connected with science: it is however certain that the larger portion of these ill-remunerated offices have been filled by clergymen.

But a much graver charge attaches itself, if not to our clergy, certainly to those who have the distribution of ecclesiastical patronage. The richest Church in the world maintains that its funds are quite insufficient for the purposes of religion, and that our working clergy are ill-paid, and church accommodation insufficient. It calls therefore upon the nation to endow it with larger funds, and yet, while reluctant to sacrifice its own superfluities, it approves of its rich sinecures being given to reward,—not the professional service of its indefatigable parochial clergy, but those of its members who, having devoted the greater part of their time to scientific researches, have political or private interest enough to obtain such advancement.

But this mode of rewarding merit is neither creditable to the Church nor advantageous to science. It tempts into the Church talents which some of its distinguished members maintain to be naturally of a disqualifying, if not of an antagonistic nature to the pursuits of religion; whilst, on the other hand, it makes a most unjust and arbitrary distinction amongst men of science themselves. It precludes those who cannot conscientiously subscribe to Articles, at once conflicting and incomprehensible, from the acquisition of that preferment and that position in society, which thus in many cases, must be conferred on less scrupulous, and certainly less distinguished inquirers into the works of nature.

As the honorary distinctions of orders of knighthood are not usually bestowed on the clerical

profession, its members generally profess to entertain a great contempt for them, and pronounce
them unfit for the recognition of scientific merit.

The want of an order for the reward of civil
service, having been publicly commented upon, the
question was at last forced upon the attention of
the government. A plan was drawn up for the
reformation of the Order of the Bath, and amongst
the qualifications for its civil grades the word science
was for the first time introduced. The draft, however, remained in the office, and the intention, if
such it were, of the Tories was not followed out.

On the advent of the Whigs to office, they seized
upon so plausible an opportunity for gaining
popularity, whilst in reality they were serving their
own purposes. They proceeded to reconstruct the
Order of the Bath, making two divisions, the Military and the Civil, each of which consisted of three
classes.

On the 25th May, 1847, there appeared in the
Gazette letters patent under the great seal recon-
stituting the Order of the Bath. It was announced
that it should consist of two divisions, the Military
and the Civil ; each division comprising three
classes. This memorable document was accompanied by certain regulations as to the number
of each class of the knights, followed by a new set
of thirty-seven statutes, which it declares *"shall
" henceforth be inviolably observed and kept within*

" *the said Order.*" But throughout these "*in-violable*" statutes, *scientific* merit is not even mentioned as a qualification.

In the Civil branch of the Order the qualification for the first class is prescribed by the eighth statute, and the tenth and twelfth statutes distinctly refer to the same. The only qualification to be found in the statutes applicable to either of the three civil classes, is when, referring to the first class of the order, it is stated that—

" No persons shall be nominated thereto, or to
" either of the other two civil divisions of this
" Order, who shall not *by their personal services to*
" *our crown*, or *by the performance of public duties*,
" have merited our royal favour."

The first of these two qualifications includes the services in the household of the Sovereign. Now although it may be agreeable, and may even be thought desirable, that the head of the State should have means of occasionally conferring distinction upon those of its subjects in personal attendance upon it, who have undertaken and accomplished duties beyond the immediate sphere of those for which they are paid in money and by position, yet such claims are personal, not national claims. The lord-in-waiting who has been the agreeable cicerone of some foreign prince, may well be contented with the diamond ring, the costly *tabatière*, or the flattering miniature, eclipsed only by the brilliants surrounding it, which recall to his memory those hours of idleness. If the prince be also a sovereign, he may add to these gratifications, that of conferring a ribbon as a further return for the *empressement* with which the polished official has fulfilled the duties of his office. Under such circumstances he will easily acquire permission to wear that distinction in his own country : a permission which would be refused by government to the author of the most splendid scientific discovery which might shed a lustre over the age in which he lives.

If such decorations are desirable for such services, let them be confined to one or to all of the four other orders : but let one national order at least be consecrated to real merit.

The only other class who are qualified by the Statutes for the honours of the Bath, are "those who by the performance of public duties have merited our favour." This may indeed include every person who holds office, but it is clear that the intention was to exclude everybody not already receiving pay from the public.

It has been suggested that a different conclusion may be inferred from the tenth paragraph of the prefatory matter to these statutes, in which the following words occur :—

"To the due distribution of rewards amongst "such of our faithful subjects as are now or shall "hereafter become eminently distinguished by their

" loyalty and merit in the military or civil service
" of us, our heirs, and successors, or *shall other-*
" *wise have merited our favour.*"

These latter words are certainly placed with some
skill, to furnish a loophole for escape, if public
opinion should scout the limited range to which the
gratitude of the country would thus be confined by
a party, who differ only from the Tories in affecting
an admiration for knowledge which they do not feel.
It must, however, be observed that this is a mere
statement, and that no such words occur in any
statute. Besides, those who maintain that the party
in power when these statutes were issued, intended
that science or any other kind of unpaid civil merit,
should be susceptible of reward by the Order of the
Bath, except it also received pay from the country,
must at the same time admit that during the four
years in which that party has distributed those
honours, England has not furnished one single
instance of any other than a paid official having
been thought sufficiently distinguished to deserve
the honour.

The public recollect with sufficient disgust the
professions of both parties especting science and
literature, when the " pension list" was revised in
1838.   The claims of science and of literature were
then with affected generosity put forward by party,
while the true object was to save for their own
advantage as large a pension list as they could.   That

object once attained, a different view of those claims was taken, as we see by its results, of which a searching analysis must at no distant day be made.

The statements uttered in both Houses even during the last session, by members of the present administration, have been so *extraordinary*, that the public are compelled to look beyond the plain English meaning of words, and to withhold their confidence until they have examined them with the scrutiny of a casuist. It is not therefore surprising that those who interpret statutes issued by such parties, should suspect the existence of latent meanings.

Dismissing this point, however, the obvious interpretation of the *statutes* of the Bath is that no one is qualified to become a member who has not been actually in the *service* of the country, that is, who has not already been paid for his labours.

The real intention of the concoctors of this scheme is too evident to be concealed. They hoped, by bestowing the Order in few and rare cases on some public servants who had made exertions beyond those of their class, or sacrifices beyond necessity, to get credit for a generosity to which they are strangers, whilst the real object was to secure for their own party and supporters the largest possible share of the patronage.

The advantages they promised themselves from the present arrangement were these : —

1st. By confining the Order of the Bath to officials, they limited the number of competitors.

2d. They thus limited it to a class which contained already a large proportion of their own friends and of the friends of their opponents.

3d. This plan enabled them, by putting into office their own connexions, persons perhaps of very ordinary abilities, ultimately to push them into the upper departments, and then on pretence of extraordinary service to give them these honours.

4th. It enabled them also to make way for such connexions, by tempting those above them, whether friends or opponents, to retire on the receipt of one or other of the decorations of the Bath.

It is not to be denied that such rewards, fairly and judiciously given for *great* and *extraordinary* services, might furnish fit motives for extraordinary exertions. But if honours are to be given to every chief of an office or head of a department, after more or less service in proportion to the extent of his political interest, or to every minister we send abroad, without regard to the success of his mission; and if promotion in the Order is to depend on the time during which they have been members of it, then the Bath will no longer be the reward of great exertions or of brilliant talent, but of seniority and routine. Its crimson ribbon will thus cease to distinguish civil merit, and become the appropriate reward of *red-tape* mediocrity.

It has been suggested that a new order of knighthood should be created, for the purpose of rewarding scientific and literary merit. This plan is entirely inadmissible : there are already five Orders of English Knights, and the new Order would, as the most recent creation, be inferior in rank to those now existing. It would, therefore, necessarily fix science at a low point in the social scale.

If it were adopted, the numerous members of the Order of the Bath would then look down upon and disparage the new Order; whilst, on the other hand, if great discoveries in science were admitted as claims to its honours, every member of the Order of the Bath would be interested in defending his scientific brethren.

§ Much discussion has lately arisen respecting the payment of persons in the employment of government. The economists have lately had a committee of the House of Commons, in which they have in some instances damaged a good cause by want of information. Their enemies will doubtless take advantage of their ignorance, and seem not unwilling to have allowed them to fall into these mistakes.

Those who contend that persons in office are under-paid, generally maintain the doctrine that the holder of every office ought to receive enough to support him, without any assistance from private fortune, in that position of society which others in the same or similar offices occupy.

This may be true for some of the higher stations, where great talents and industry are essential; but these offices are the exceptions. To maintain this doctrine is to assert, that the government must pay such a salary to every employé as to be able to choose out of the whole number of persons existing in the country, those most capable of filling that office. Now in every country where capital has at all accumulated, there will always be a sufficient number of persons, having some amount of private fortune, who will be able and willing to fill all the ordinary offices requiring no very special talent, for a much smaller sum than their average expenditure would require. This more limited class is yet sufficiently large for the government to select from. The competition of capital with labour leads to this result.

The inducements to office under government are many, in addition to that of its salary.

1st. The salary itself generally increases with the time of service.

2d. There is usually a retiring pension after a certain time of service, or in case of accidental incapacity.

3d. There is the chance of promotion by political interest, or perchance from skill and industry displayed in office.

4th. Some incapable head of a department may want a clever fellow to do the work for which he is himself either too idle or too ignorant.

5th. There is the chance of being promoted, in order to make a vacancy for some one below who has more influence.

6th. Then there are the great prizes,—few indeed, but very great when occurring to those without the accidents of birth or interest. It is possible that a clerk commencing at a salary of 80*l.* may ultimately attain a seat in the cabinet, and then the peerage is open to him.

Admitting that there are several cases in which offices are considerably underpaid, no answer has yet been given to the great argument arising from supply and demand. It is an admitted fact, that for every office under government, and for every grade in the army and navy, the number of fitting candidates on each vacancy is very large, and the political and family interest set at work to acquire it, is very great. This can arise only from those offices being overpaid, not by the actual money payment, but by combining that form of remuneration with position in society, and other advantages to which they lead. If this be the case, it is quite unnecessary to add any new inducement—such as the decoration of the Bath—to those so circumstanced, unless it be indeed for very extraordinary services.

Another indication of over-payment is to be found in the fact, that in several professions such offices are matter of sale and purchase. They are so avowedly both in the Church and in the Army.

The Whigs, afraid of intellect when combined with independence, have, during their temporary and tolerated possession of office, confined the new honours the country has to bestow, to those persons only who can be influenced by the hope of promotion,—namely, to those already occupying office. If a distinction is to be made amongst scientific men, let us inquire whether those who fill the few public situations reserved for science and paid by the country, ought to be eligible rather than those whose equally successful contributions to science have been given without any such advantage.

To enable any individual in the present day to enlarge the bounds of science by original discovery, he must be content to sacrifice his whole time and energies to that object. It is true that a considerable or even a great knowledge of certain sciences, and possibly the power of making some additions to them, may co-exist in a few instances with the qualifications necessary for other employments. Such attainments are highly creditable to those officials who so employ their leisure without neglecting their official duties. But the more successful their scientific discoveries, the greater must be the regret that the whole power of such intelligence cannot be directed to one subject.

The various sciences have, it is true, such relations to each other, that few can be cultivated to any great advantage without some acquaintance with those sciences intimately connected with the favourite pursuit. But if it is admitted that all inquiries into Nature and her laws, are directly beneficial to the arts and commerce of the country, it is, in a national point of view, eminently impolitic not to secure for science that division of labour which so remarkably contributes to the progress of all other subjects.

In addition to the unbounded occupation of time and thought, necessary for the most effective employment of mind in the path of original discovery, there are far other requisites. In some sciences, many laborious transcriptions, in others still more laborious arithmetical computations, are required; in others, abstruse and complicated although known and regulated algebraical processes, must be gone through; in others, drawings of the most complicated description must be executed with almost overwhelming labour; in others, extensive experiments must be made. Again, in some, where mechanical means must be contrived for new and intellectual processes, it may be necessary even to invent and make new tools for the purpose of bringing mechanical art itself up to that degree of perfec-

tion which science demands. Although the contriving and directing mind engaged in researches
that require such aids, ought undoubtedly to be
united with a physical structure capable itself of
accomplishing each and all that such pursuits require, yet it is often impossible that one human
frame, however hardy, can sustain that labour:
time itself would be wanting, limited as it ever
must be by the duration of one human life.

Yet if the powers of that mind and that frame
have been rightly cultivated, and if the want of
pecuniary means do not prevent their exercise, it is
quite possible, by proper aid, to concentrate in one
life the accumulated labour of many. Assistants of
various degrees of manual and mental skill may be
employed, the economical organization of their
labour may be arranged. The most perfect effect
of such an establishment can only be attained when
the presiding head is never employed except on
work for which money could procure no substitute, and when each assistant is devoted to work
of the highest kind which he can successfully
execute.

He who directs a scientific establishment for the
Government, has all these means provided for him,
and is himself paid, though not always liberally, for
his own labours. *He* is to be deemed *qualified* for
the order of the Bath.

He who sacrifices profession and that position to

which its most successful members usually attain, who spends a fortune in purchasing that assistance which alone can render his power effective, and has spent his life in cultivating highly that power for the advancement of science, is deemed by his country, however great his success, *disqualified* for the Order of the Bath.

But it is not the sound and wholesome part of the country—it is not the people of England who have arrived at this conclusion ;—it is the insolence of power,—it is the meanness of party,—it is the selfishness of a clique.

The spirit which dictated a limitation equally opposed to every generous feeling and to every statesman-like view, is consistent only with such influences. When the ministry founded that new source of patronage, it sought to acquire for itself a kind of popularity amongst its adherents. Had it admitted intellectual merit, it would have obtained popularity for the Crown from an enlightened nation. But the interests of party are transitory,— those of the sovereign permanent : it is the interest of party to be ever jealous of the personal popularity of the Crown.

In thus excluding from its honours one class of the intelligence of the country, did it never occur to the short-sighted minister who planned this arrangement, that some portion of the talents thus insulted, might be driven to other inquiries which it would

neither be easy to answer nor even expedient to
discuss ?

A party which first refuses to science the means
of acquiring competence,—then excludes it from
personal honours because it has already been denied
official position,—and which refuses it hereditary
rank, because it has not devoted itself to the acquisition of wealth, will naturally cause questions to
be raised as to the expediency of different forms of
government.

Of what class, it will naturally be asked, are the
persons who have made such laws ?

Is the possession of hereditary rank at all necessary for the government of the country ?

At a.distant period, and under a less complicated
form of society, the obvious disadvantages of appointing a legislator for life from the accident of his
birth, instead of the fitness of his talents, might
have been tolerated under the influence of force.
It has since been consecrated by established usage,
and some of its evils mitigated by the continual
infusion of fresh blood into decaying stocks.   But
at the present day, and amidst the multiplied
relations of highly civilized life, the question
whether an upper chamber ought to be hereditary,
or appointed only for life, is one upon which nations
as well as philosophers, avowedly disagree.

In a very few years this great question will
come to be more thoroughly investigated, and

those who now advocate the continuance of existing institutions, will then have enough on their hands, without rashly forcing, by injustice and insult, both talent and interest into the ranks of their opponents.

At present it is sufficient to call attention to a statement often made, that a chamber of Peers for life is incompatible with the existence of a limited monarchy. This, like many other party dogmas, is a mere gratuitous assertion, put forward to alarm the timid who have experienced the advantages and are anxious for the continuance of that form of government.

Various opinions have been advanced, and are current in society, concerning the proper reward for those *whose science adds to the boundaries of human knowledge*, and certain principles are held by the occupiers of high political office, to which it may be well to advert.

Some of these persons have themselves acquired a smattering of one science, political economy, and thus they reason :—They are informed that it is a highly agreeable occupation to make discoveries, and although it is known that it costs years of labour and study to acquire that power, yet it is found that many persons are willing to indulge in this luxury, and are generally disposed to publish the results of their discoveries. Since, therefore, the public can get the benefit of the knowledge for nothing, it would be very extravagant in the stewards of the public to pay anything for it.

But it seems not to have been observed by these reasoners, that although all discoveries are of value to the country, yet the time at which they become practically useful occurs at very different, and often at distant periods. It might also be suggested to them, that the discoverers of the great principles of nature are very rarely the persons most capable of applying them to practice. It is also clear that the acquisition of money was not one of their objects in devoting themselves to such unprofitable pursuits.

Under such circumstances, if the Government neither encourage science by pecuniary nor by honorary reward, it is most probable that the discoveries which are made, will occur in its more recondite recesses ; and as the only recompense obtained is the intellectual pleasure felt in the pursuit, the greater part of the discoveries made will be of the most abstract kind.

This tendency is still further increased by the fact that the far larger number of those who cultivate science, are precluded from competition by the expense necessary for the pursuit of many of its more practical branches. The most highly intellectual and exciting,—all the departments of the pure mathematics, for example, attract by the comparative economy of the expenditure they demand.

And yet it may happen that immense sums might have been saved to the nation, if the efforts of competent men had been applied to reform the domestic economy or rather the domestic extravagance of many of our public establishments, instead of expending them more agreeably though less profitably, on the interpretation of an almost impossible cypher, or the still more interesting discovery of relations amongst new orders of imaginary quantities.

How often has the question been asked by persons seeking a profitable investment of their capital, Will such a canal or railroad pay? This is really an indefinite question, and admits of no one answer applicable to all cases. It may, for example, in some particular instance, be tolerably certain that at the end of the first four years, if the shares are sold, and the account closed, there will be an entire loss of half the principal, and all interest during that time. If the shares are not sold until the end of eight years, they will produce a return of the original capital, together with a profit of five per cent. If, however, those shares were retained until the end of twelve years, they might, when sold, produce a return of the original capital, together with a profit of ten per cent. during the whole time.

Now, it is obvious that the answer to the question, "Will that canal or railway pay?" must depend on the capital possessed by the purchaser and on the period of time during which he can afford to abstain from its use. The purchaser who could not abstain from the use of the interest of his money for four years might be ruined, whilst he who could abstain for twelve, might be greatly enriched. But a wealthy country is generally better able to abstain than any commercial firm, and the investment in discoveries becoming productive at a distant time, will be of far more advantage to a nation than to individuals.

A certain number of persons maintain the opinion, that if men of science became rich they would become idle, and that it is expedient to starve them into discovery. Such persons may perhaps have been misled by arguing from a supposed analogy with some other profession. But the pleasure of science arises from the exertion, not from the inactivity of the mind.

Others, and a very large number, hold that science is of so sublime a nature, that it ought to be above all sublunary rewards;—they maintain that it is beneath its dignity to wish for the wealth or the honours awarded to success in other pursuits; —that ribbons and titles are quite unworthy of the ambition of those who are searching into the truths of nature.

When men state a principle, the best test of their sincerity is to be found in their application of it.

We may ourselves utterly repudiate a principle, and yet be unable to show that it is not sincerely believed by those who assert its authority.   Man cannot dive into the mind of his fellow-man, and witness the internal conviction he asserts; but he can always examine the *fairness* with which he applies that principle.

Now, if the lofty dignity of science is such that it is, from its very nature, incompatible with wealth—if decorations and titles are entirely unworthy of its legitimate ambition,—then, as a necessary consequence, all pursuits of a higher order are still more absolutely excluded from such vanities.

Is it consistent, therefore, with these opinions, to maintain that the Ministers of a Christian Church, who interpret to us the *word* of God, should receive payment for their labour, rank for their exertions, and, in some instances, even the very ribbons* so

---

* The following dignitaries of the Church wear decorations of Orders of Knighthood.

Archbishop of Armagh.	Bishop of Oxford.
Archbishop of Dublin.	Dean of Westminster.
Dean of St. Patrick.	

The vestments of the Bishop of Oxford throw into the shade those even of Roman Catholic prelates.

" The said prelate shall have and wear for his habit, a " mantle of crimson velvet, lined with white taffeta, richly " guarded with the Sovereign's badges and cognizances, and " upon his right shoulder an escutcheon of the arms of the

contemned : whilst those who make us intimately acquainted with the *works* of the Almighty, who discover to us the laws which he has impressed on matter, and thus add to the physical comfort, the intellectual pleasure, and the religious feeling of mankind, should be compelled to exercise those rare endowments, only by the sacrifice of fortune and the renunciation of all those enjoyments, rewards, and honours, which the ministers even of the purest creed receive without reproach ?

But these are the opinions of the shallow and the thoughtless. The pursuits of mind may modify, they can never obliterate the instincts, the feelings, or the passions of man.

The consciousness of power, and the conviction of its successful exertion, exist undiminished by the neglect or the ingratitude of the country he inhabits. The certainty that a future age will repair the injustice of the present, and the knowledge that the more distant the day of reparation, the more he has outstripped the efforts of his cotemporaries, may well sustain him against the sneers of the ignorant, or the jealousy of rivals.

It is possible that in some rare instance such a man may feel personally little ambition to attain what all others covet; still, however, he may be

" Order, within a garter, and the lace of his mantle shall be " of blue silk, interwoven with gold."—*History of British Orders of Knighthood, by Sir Harris Nicolas,* p. 430.

bound by other ties which link him inseparably to the present.

He may look with fond and affectionate gratitude on her whose maternal care watched over the dangers of his childhood; who trained his infant mind, and with her own mild power, checking the rash vigour of his youthful days, remained ever the faithful and respected counsellor of his riper age. To gladden the declining years of her who with more than prophetic inspiration, foresaw as woman only can, the distant fame of her beloved offspring, he may well be forgiven the desire for some outward mark of his country's approbation.

If such a relative were wanting, there might yet survive another parent whose less enthusiastic temperament had ever repressed those fond anticipations of maternal affection, but who now in the ripeness of his honoured age, might be compelled, with faltering accents, to admit that the voice of the country confirmed the predictions of the mother.

Perhaps another and yet dearer friend might exist, the partner of his daily cares, the witness of his unceasing toil; whose youthful mind, cultivated by his skill, rewards with enduring affection those efforts which called into existence her own latent and unsuspected powers. When driven by exhausted means and injured health almost to despair of the achievement of his life's great object—when the brain itself reels beneath the weight its own ambition has imposed, and the world's neglect aggravates the throbbings of an overtasked frame, an angel spirit sits beside his couch ministering with gentlest skill to every wish, watching with anxious thought till renovated nature shall admit of bolder counsels, then points the way to hope, herself the guardian of his deathless fame.

The fool may sneer, the worldly-wise may smile, the heartless laugh,—the saint may moralize, the bigot preach : there dwells not within the deep recesses of the human heart one sentiment more powerful, more exalted, or more pure than these.

That man is not a statesman, who is unaware of the strength of these powerful excitements to human action. Cold and incapable of such sentiments himself,—no grasp of intellect enables him to infer their existence, and thus to supply the deficiencies of his own, by an insight into the hearts of others.

That man is a fool, not a statesman, who knowing their strength, hesitates to avail himself of it for the benefit of his country and of mankind.

But if there should arise a man conscious of their power, who yet should dare to use it for the purposes of party, that man will combine in his character the not incongruous mixture of statesman and of knave. A statesman he may be, if he can penetrate into the character of men, and can divine the action of human motives upon the masses, as well as on the individuals of his race. With such knowledge, and with the talent that its possession implies, he cannot be a fool; except indeed, in as far as he is entitled to credit for that limited amount of folly which is inseparably attached to him in his other character of knave. It is *possible* that he may be successful in his day; it is *certain* that he will ultimately be found out and disgraced in the eyes of posterity. His name may remain a beacon for a time, until some greater or more recent knave supersedes his example, and thus consigns him to oblivion.

It is not then the gaudy ribbon, the brilliant star, the titled name, that have intrinsic charms for him who dedicates his genius to the search for truth. How large a portion of his real greatness, even of his most splendid discoveries, would he not willingly sacrifice to confer on those he loves that exquisite happiness, which arises only when hidden but long-cherished convictions, entertained diffidently from the consciousness of partial affection, receive at length their final confirmation by that decision which national acknowledgment can alone command!

Appendix.

THE

ELEVENTH CHAPTER

OF THE

HISTORY OF THE ROYAL SOCIETY.

BY

C. R. WELD, ESQ.

ASSISTANT SECRETARY OF THE ROYAL SOCIETY.

REPRINTED WITH THE PERMISSION OF THE PROPRIETOR.

HISTORY OF THE ROYAL SOCIETY.

CHAPTER XI.

The Society receive a Letter from the Treasury respecting Mr.
Babbage's Calculating Machine—Letter from Mr. Babbage to
Sir H. Davy—A Committee appointed to consider Mr. Babbage's
Plan—They Report in favour of it—Mr. Babbage has an interview
with the Chancellor of the Exchequer—Government advance
1,500l.—Difference-Engine commenced—Mr. Babbage gives all his
labour gratuitously—Advice of the Society again requested—Mr.
Babbage's Statement—Committee appointed to inspect the Engine
—Their Report—Heavy Expenses not met by the Treasury—
Meeting of Mr. Babbage's personal friends — Their Report—
Duke of Wellington inspects the Works — His Grace recom-
mends the Treasury to make further Payments—Letter from
Mr. Babbage to the Treasury — Communication from the Trea-
sury to the Council — Referred to a Committee — Report of
Committee—They recommend the Works to be removed to the
vicinity of Mr. Babbage's Residence—Government act on the
Recommendation—Fire-pooof Buildings erected—Misunderstand-
ing with Mr. Clement—Works stopped—Mr. Babbage discovers
new principles which supersede those connected with the Difference-Engine—He requests an interview with Lord Melbourne—
Letter to M. Quetelet explaining the principles of Analytical-
Engine—Mr. Babbage visits Turin—M. Menabrea's account of the
Engine—Translated with Notes by Lady Lovelace—Mr. Babbage
applies to Government for their Determination—Letter from the
Chancellor of the Exchequer—Mr. Babbage's Answer—Government
resolve not to proceed with the Engine—Mr. Babbage has an
interview with Sir R. Peel—Difference-Engine placed in the
Museum of King's College—Present State of the Analytical-
Engine.

1820-25.

ON the 1st April, 1823, a letter was received from
the Treasury, requesting the Council to take into
consideration a plan which had been submitted to
Government by Mr. Babbage, for "applying machinery

to the purposes of calculating and printing mathematical
tables ;" and the Lords of the Treasury further desired
" to be favoured with the opinion of the Royal Society
on the merits and utility of this invention[1]."

This is the earliest allusion to the celebrated Calculating Engine of Mr. Babbage, in the records of the
Society[2].   But the invention had been brought before
them in the previous year by a letter from Mr. Babbage
to Sir H. Davy, dated July 3, 1822, in which he gives
some account of a small model of his engine for calculating differences, which " produced figures at the rate
of 44 a minute, and performed with rapidity and precision all those calculations for which it was designed[3]."
He then proceeds to enumerate various tables which
the machine was adapted to calculate, and concludes :
" I am aware that these statements may perhaps be
viewed as something more than Utopian, and that the
philosophers of Laputa may be called up to dispute my

---

[1] In the following account of the Difference and Analytical Engines,
besides the MS. documents in the Archives of the Royal Society, I have
derived very valuable information from an unpublished statement
drawn up by Mr. Babbage, which he has been so kind as to place in my
hands.   The original documents which are in Mr. Babbage's possession,
and which are referred to, I have myself examined.

[2] The idea of a Calculating Engine is not new.   The celebrated
Pascal constructed a machine for executing the ordinary operations of
arithmetic, a description of which will be found in the *Encycl. Méthod.*,
and in the Works of Pascal, Tom. IV. p. 7, Paris, 1819.   In his *Pensées*
he says, alluding to this Engine : " *La machine arithmétique fait des
effets qui approchent plus de la pensée que tout ce que font les animaux ;
mais elle ne fait rien qui puisse faire dire qu'elle a de la volonté comme
les animaux.*"   Subsequently, Leibnitz invented a machine by which,
says Mr. De Morgan, " arithmetic computations could be made."
Polenus, a learned and ingenious Italian, invented a machine by which
multiplication was performed—and mechanical contrivances for performing particular arithmetical processes were made about a century
ago, but they were merely modifications of Pascal's.   These Engines
were very different to Mr. Babbage's Difference-Engine.

[3] This letter was printed and published in July, 1822.

claim to originality.   Should such be the case, I hope
the resemblance will be found to adhere to the nature
of the subject, rather than to the manner in which it
has been treated.   Conscious from my own experience
of the difficulty of convincing those who are but little
skilled in mathematical knowledge, of the possibility of
making a machine which shall perform calculations, I
was naturally anxious, in introducing it to the public,
to appeal to the testimony of one so distinguished in
the records of British science[4].   Induced by a conviction of the great utility of such engines, to withdraw
for some time my attention from a subject on which it
has been engaged during several years, and which possesses charms of a higher order, I have now arrived at
a point where success is no longer doubtful.   It must,
however, be attained at a very considerable expense,
which would not probably be replaced by the works it
might produce for a long period of time, and which is
an undertaking I should feel unwilling to commence, as
altogether foreign to my habits and pursuits."

The Council appointed a Committee to take Mr.
Babbage's plan into consideration, which was composed
of the following gentlemen: Sir H. Davy, Mr. Brande,
Mr. Combe, Mr. Baily, Mr. (now Sir Mark Isambard)
Brunel, Major (now General) Colby, Mr. Davies Gilbert, Mr. (now Sir John) Herschel, Captain Kater,
Mr. Pond (Astronomer-Royal), Dr. Wollaston, and
Dr. Young.   On the 1st May, 1823, the Committee
reported: " That it appears that Mr. Babbage has displayed great talents and ingenuity in the construction
of his machine for computation, which the Committee
think fully adequate to the attainment of the objects

---

[4] Sir H. Davy had witnessed and expressed his admiration of the
performances of the Engine.

proposed by the inventor, and that they consider Mr. Babbage as highly deserving of public encouragement in the prosecution of his arduous undertaking[5]."

This Report was transmitted to the Lords of the Treasury, by whom it was, with Mr. Babbage's letter to Sir H. Davy, printed and laid before Parliament[6].

In July, 1823, Mr. Babbage had an interview with the Chancellor of the Exchequer, Mr. Robinson (now Earl of Ripon), to ascertain if it were the wish of Government that he should construct a large engine of the kind, which would also print the results it calculated. Unfortunately, no Minute of that conversation was made at the time, nor was any sufficiently distinct understanding arrived at, as it afterwards appeared that a contrary impression was left on the mind of either party[7]. Mr. Babbage's conviction was, that whatever might be the labour and difficulty of the undertaking, the engine itself would, of course, become the property of the Government, which had paid for its construction.

Soon after this interview with the Chancellor of the Exchequer, a letter was sent from the Treasury to the Royal Society, informing them that the Lords of the Treasury "had directed the issue of 1,500*l.* to Mr. Babbage, to enable him to bring his invention to perfection, in the manner recommended."

These words "*in the manner recommended*," can refer

---

[5] I am informed upon good authority, that Dr. Young differed in opinion from his colleagues. Without doubting that an engine could be made, he conceived that it would be far more useful to invest the probable cost of constructing such a calculating machine as was proposed, in the funds, and apply the dividends to paying calculators.

[6] Parliamentary Paper, No. 370, 1823.

[7] Mr. Babbage very justly observes, that had the mutual relations of the two parties, and the details of the plans then adopted, been clearly defined, there is little doubt but that the Difference-Engine would long since have existed.

only to the previous recommendation by the Royal Society; but it does not appear from their Report, that any plan, terms, or conditions had been pointed out.

Towards the end of July, 1823, Mr. Babbage took measures for the construction of the present Difference-Engine[8], and it was regularly proceeded with for four years.

And here it is right to state, that Mr. Babbage gave his mental labour gratuitously, and that from first to last he has not derived any emolument whatever from Government[9]. Sectional, and other drawings, of the most delicate nature had to be made; tools to be formed expressly to meet mechanical difficulties; and workmen to be educated in the practical knowledge necessary in the construction of the machine. The mechanical department was placed under the management of Mr. Clement, a draughtsman of great ability, and a practical mechanic of the highest order[10]. Money was advanced from time to time by the Treasury, the accounts furnished by the engineer undergoing the examination of auditors[11], and passing through the hands of Mr.

---

[8] It will be desirable to distinguish between,
1. The small *Model* of the Original or Difference-Engine.
2. The Difference-Engine itself, belonging to the Government, a part only of which has been put together.
3. The designs for another Engine called the Analytical-Engine.

[9] Sir R. Peel distinctly admitted this in the House of Commons in March, 1843.

[10] A curious anecdote is related illustrative of the great perfection to which Mr. Clement was in the habit of bringing machinery. He received an order from America to construct a large screw in the *best possible manner,* and he accordingly made one with the greatest mathematical accuracy. But his bill amounted to some hundreds of pounds, which completely staggered the American, who never calculated upon paying more than 20*l.* at the utmost for the screw. The matter was referred to arbitrators, who gave an opinion in favour of Mr. Clement.

[11] They were Messrs. Brunel, Donkin, and Field.

Babbage.   Thus years elapsed, and public attention
became at length directed to the fact, that a large sum
had been expended upon the construction of the engine,
which was not completed.   Again the advice of the
Royal Society was solicited.

In December, 1828, Government begged the Council
" to institute such enquiries as would enable them to
report upon the state to which it (the machine) had
then arrived; and also whether the progress made in
its construction confirmed them in the opinion which
they had formerly expressed, that it would ultimately
prove adequate to the important object which it was
intended to attain."

Accompanying this communication was a statement
from Mr. Babbage of the condition of the engine, in
which he says:—

" The machine has required a longer time and greater
expense than was anticipated, and Mr. Babbage has already
expended about 6,000l. on this object. The work is now in
a state of considerable forwardness, numerous and large drawings of it have been made, and much of the mechanism has
been executed, and many workmen are occupied daily in its
completion."

A Committee was appointed by the Council, con-
sisting of Mr. Gilbert (President), Dr. Roget, Captain
Sabine, Sir John Herschel, Mr. Baily, Mr. Brunel,
Captain Kater, Mr. Donkin, Mr. Penn, Mr. Rennie,
Mr. Barton, and Mr. Warburton.[12]

They minutely inspected the drawings, tools, and
the parts of the engine then executed, and drew up a
report, " declining to consider the principle on which
the practicability of the machinery depends, and of the

---

[12] Colonel Sabine informs me, that Dr. Whewell was afterwards added
to the Committee.

public utility of the object which it proposes to attain ;
because they considered the former fully admitted, and
the latter obvious to all who consider the immense
advantage of accurate numerical tables in all matters of
calculation, which it is professedly the object of the
engine to calculate and print with perfect accuracy."

They further stated, that " the progress made was
as great as could be expected, considering the numerous
difficulties to be overcome ; and lastly, that they had
no hesitation in giving it as their opinion, that the
engine was likely to fulfil the expectations entertained
of it by its inventor."

The Council adopted the Report, expressing their
trust, that while Mr. Babbage's mind was intently
occupied on an undertaking likely to do so much
honour to his country, he might be relieved as much
as possible from all other sources of anxiety.

It is clear that the Council of the Royal Society
regarded Mr. Babbage's engine, as it then existed, in a
favourable light, and were sanguine respecting its
satisfactory completion.

Government acted on the foregoing Report ; funds
were advanced, the machinery was declared national
property, and the works were continued.   But there
was evidently a misgiving on the part of the Lords of
the Treasury, for the official payments soon failed to
meet the heavy and increasing expenses incurred by
Mr. Babbage.

Under these circumstances, by the advice of Mr.
Wolryche Whitmore (Mr. Babbage's brother-in-law),
a meeting of Mr. Babbage's personal friends was held
on the 12th of May, 1829.   It consisted of:—

The Duke of Somerset, F.R.S.,
Lord Ashley, M.P.,
Sir John Franklin, Capt. R.N., F.R.S.,

s 2

Mr. Wolryche Whitmore, M.P.,
Dr. Fitton, F.R.S.,
Mr. Francis Baily, F.R.S.,
Sir John Herschel, F.R.S.

They drew up the annexed Report :—

" *May* 12, 1829.

" The attention of the undersigned personal friends of Mr. Babbage having been called by him to the actual state of his Machine for Calculating and Printing Mathematical Tables; and to his relation to the Government on the one hand, and to the Engineers and workmen employed by him in its execution on the other, declare themselves satisfied, from his statements and from the documents they have perused, of the following facts.

" That Mr. Babbage was originally induced to take up the work on its present extensive scale, by an understanding on his part, that it was the wish of Government he should do so, and by an advance of 1,500*l.* in the outset, with a full impression on his mind that such further advances would be made as the progress of the work should require, and as should secure him from ultimate loss.

" That the public and scientific importance of the Engine has been acknowledged, in a Report of a Committee of the Royal Society, made at the time of its first receiving the sanction of His Majesty's Government, and that its actual state of progress is such, as in the opinion of the most eminent Engineers and other Members of the Royal Society, as detailed in a further Report of a Committee of that body, to warrant their impression of the moral certainty of its success, should funds not be wanting for its completion.

" That it appears, that Mr. Babbage's actual expenditure has amounted to nearly 7,000*l.* and that the whole sum advanced to him by the Government is 3,000*l.*

" That Mr. Babbage has devoted, from the commencement of his arduous undertaking, the most assiduous and anxious attention to the work in hand, to the injury of his health, and the neglect and refusal of other profitable occupations.

" That a very large expense still remains to be incurred, to the probable amount of at least 4,000*l.*, as far as he can foresee, before the Engine can be completed; but that Mr. Babbage's private fortune is not such as, in their opinion, to justify the sacrifices he must make in completing it without further and effectual assistance from Government; taking into consideration not only his own interest, but that of his family dependent on him.

" Under these circumstances, it is their opinion that a full and speedy representation of the case ought to be made to Government, and that in the most direct manner by a personal application to his Grace the Duke of Wellington.

" And that in case of such application proving unsuccessful in procuring effectual and adequate assistance, they must regard Mr. Babbage as no longer called on—considering the pecuniary and personal sacrifices he will then have made; considering the entire and *bonâ fide* expenditure of all that he will have received from the public purse on the object of its destination, and considering the moral certainty to which it is at length by his exertions reduced—as no longer called on to go on with an undertaking which may prove the destruction of his health, and the great injury, if not the ruin of his fortune.

" That it is their opinion that Mr. W. Whitmore and Mr. Herschel should request an interview with the Duke of Wellington for the purpose of making this representation.

(Signed,)   " Somerset.
                              " Ashley.
                              " John Franklin.
                              " W. W. Whitmore.
                              " Wm. Henry Fitton.
                              " Francis Baily.
                              " J. F. W. Herschel."

In consequence of what passed at this interview, which took place as suggested, the Duke of Wellington, accompanied by the Chancellor of the Exchequer (Mr. Goulburn) and Lord Ashley, inspected the *model* of the engine, the drawings, and parts in progress. The Duke recommended that a grant of 3,000*l.* should be made towards the completion of the machine, which was duly paid by the Treasury.

In the mean time, difficulties of another kind arose. The engineer, who had constructed the Engine under Mr. Babbage's directions, had delivered his bills in such a state, that it was impossible to judge how far the charges were just and reasonable ; and although Mr. Babbage had paid several thousand pounds, there yet remained a considerable balance, which could not be liquidated until the accounts had been examined, and the charges approved by professional engineers.

With a view of drawing attention to these charges, Mr. Babbage addressed the following letter to the Chancellor of the Exchequer :—

" *Dorset Street*, 21 *December*, 1830.

" MY LORD,

" I beg to call your Lordship's attention to the enclosed account[13] of the expenses of the Machine for calculating and printing mathematical tables, by which it appears that a sum of 592*l*. 4*s*. 8*d*. remained due to myself upon the last account, and that a further sum of nearly 600*l*. has since become due to Mr. Clement.

" It is for the payment of this latter sum that I wish to call your Lordship's attention. Mr. Maudslay, one of the engineers appointed by the Government to examine the bills of Mr. Clement, having been unable from illness to attend, his report has been delayed, and Mr. Clement informs me that should the money remain unpaid much longer, he shall

	£	s.	d.
[13] Expense to end of 1824	600	0	0
Ditto „ „ 1827	521	16	9
Mr. Clement's Bills to June, 1827	4,775	15	3
Ditto, 9th May, 1829	730	12	8
	6,628	4	8
Deduct old tools sold	36	0	0
	6,592	4	8
Mr. Clement's Bill to December, 1830, *about*	600	0	0
	7,192	4	8

be obliged, from want of funds, to discharge some of the
workmen ; an event which I need not inform your Lordship
would be very prejudicial to the progress of the machine.

" Another point which I wish to submit to your attention,
when your Lordship shall have had leisure to examine personally the present state of the works, is, that since it is
absolutely necessary to find additional room for the erection
of the machine, it becomes a matter of serious consideration
whether it would not contribute to the speedier completion of
the machine, and also to economy in expenditure, to remove
the works to the neighbourhood of my own residence.

" I have, &c.

" C. BABBAGE."

The receipt of this letter caused the Treasury to
make the following communication to the Secretary of
the Royal Society :—

" SIR,   " Treasury, 24 December, 1830.
          " The Lords Commissioners of H. M. Treasury,
having had under their consideration a letter from Mr.
Babbage, containing an account of the expense which has
been incurred in the construction of the Machine for calculating and printing mathematical tables, amounting to the sum
of 7,192l. 4s. 8d., and requesting an advance of 600l. to
defray a part of that expense ; I am commanded by their
Lordships to refer you to the Report of the Council of the
Royal Society dated 16th February, 1829, which entirely
satisfied their Lordships of the propriety of supporting Mr.
Babbage in the construction of this machine, and to state
that advances to the amount of 6,000l. have been made on
this account, and that directions have been given for a further
advance of 600l.

" I am also to acquaint you, that the Machine is the property of Government, and consequently my Lords propose to
defray the further expense necessary for its completion.   I am
further to request you will move the Council of the Royal
Society to cause the machine to be inspected, and to favour
my Lords with their opinion whether the work is proceeding

in a satisfactory manner, and without unnecessary expense, and what further sum may probably be necessary for completing it.

" I am, &c.

" The Secretary, Royal Society."   " J. STEWART."

The consideration of this letter was referred to the same Committee which had previously been appointed for a similar purpose, with the addition of Sir John Lubbock and Mr. Troughton.

Again the Committee met[14] Mr. Babbage, at No. 21, Prospect Place, Lambeth (where the construction of the engine was carried on), and minutely inspected the machinery and drawings.

Their Report embodied the whole facts of the case:— the workmanship of the various parts of the machine was declared to have been executed with the greatest possible degree of perfection, and the pains taken to verify the charges on the part of the Government altogether satisfactory. It was recommended that the vacancy occasioned by the decease of Mr. Maudslay, who had been appointed to inspect the accounts, should be filled up by another engineer, conversant with the execution of machinery, and the value thereof. With respect to the suggested removal of the workshops nearer to Mr. Babbage's residence, the Committee gave their entire concurrence, on the ground that greater expedition would thereby be attained in carrying on the work, and that it was highly essential to secure all the machinery and drawings in fire-proof premises, without delay. A plot of ground held on lease by Mr. Babbage, adjacent to his garden at the back of his

---

[14] I have a letter of Sir J. Herschel's before me, expressing his regret at being unable to attend on this occasion, but that his faith in the engine and its inventor remained unshaken.

house in Dorset Street, was recommended as a desirable site for the contemplated erections, of which the plans and estimates had been submitted to the Committee. The framers of the Report stated in conclusion that :—

" Such an arrangement would be eminently conducive to the speedy and economical completion of the Machine, as well as to the effectual working and employment of the same, after it shall have been completed.

" That as to the sum which may be necessary for completing the Engine, they attach hereto the estimate of Mr. Brunel." [15]

The Report, with Mr. Brunel's estimate, were sent to the Treasury on the 13th April, 1831 : and having been approved by a Committee of practical engineers appointed by Government, the latter acted on the recommendations which it contained. The piece of ground adjoining Mr. Babbage's garden was taken, and a fire-proof building erected, designed to contain the plans and drawings, and also the engine when completed. But new and unforeseen difficulties arose. When about 17,000*l.* had been expended, further progress was arrested on account of a misunderstanding

---

[15] Mr. Brunel's estimate appears in the following letter to Mr. Warburton:—

" DEAR SIR,   " *Feb.* 28, 1831.

" HAVING taken in consideration the erection of the proposed shops, the removal of the machinery, the accommodation for it, and also for the maker ; having also taken into consideration the further completion of the drawings, and the ultimate accomplishment of the Engine until it is capable of producing plates for printing ; though I feel confident that the sum of 8,000*l.* will be ample to realize the objects that are contemplated, I should nevertheless recommend that the Government be advised to provide for the sum of 12,000*l.* by way of estimate, and that the yearly sum required, exclusive of the sum requisite for the buildings and removal (say 2,000*l.*), will not exceed from 2,000*l.* to 2,500*l.*

                                                    " I am, &c.

" *Henry Warburton, Esq.*"   " M. I. BRUNEL."

with Mr. Clement, who made the most extravagant
demands as compensation for carrying on the construction of the engine in the new buildings. These demands
could not be satisfied with proper regard to the justice
due to Government. Mr. Clement accordingly withdrew from the undertaking, and carried with him all
the valuable tools that had been used in the work; a
proceeding the more unfortunate, as many of them had
been invented expressly to meet the unusual forms and
combinations arising out of the novel construction.[16]

An offer was made to surrender the tools, for a given
sum, which was declined, and the works came to a
stand-still. But other circumstances interposed to prevent the completion of the original design.

During the suspension of the works, Mr. Babbage
had been deprived of the use of his own drawings.
Having in the meanwhile naturally speculated upon
the general principles on which machinery for calculation might be constructed, *a principle of an entirely
new kind* occurred to him, the power of which over the
most complicated arithmetical operations seemed nearly
unbounded. This was the executing of analytical operations by means of an analytical-engine. On re-
examining his drawings, when returned to him by the
engineer, the new principle appeared to be limited only
by the extent of the mechanism it might require.
The invention of simpler mechanical means for performing the elementary operations of the engine, now
derived a far greater importance than it had hitherto
possessed; and should such simplifications be discovered,

---

[16] This Mr. Clement had a legal right to do. Startling as it may
appear to the unprofessional reader, it is nevertheless the fact, that
engineers and mechanics possess the right of property to all tools that
they have constructed, although the cost of construction has been
defrayed by their employers.

it seemed difficult to anticipate, or even to over-estimate, the vast results which might be attained.

These new views acquired additional importance from their bearings upon the engine already partly executed for the Government; for, if such simplifications should be discovered, it might happen that the Analytical-Engine would execute with greater rapidity the calculations for which the Difference-Engine was intended; or that the Difference-Engine would itself be superseded by a far simpler mode of construction.

Though these views might perhaps at that period have appeared visionary, they have subsequently been completely realized. To have allowed the construction of the Difference-Engine to be resumed, while these new conceptions were withheld from the Government, would have been improper; yet the state of uncertainty in which those views were then necessarily involved, rendered any written communication respecting their probable bearing on that engine, a task of very great difficulty. It therefore appeared to Mr. Babbage, that the most straightforward course was to ask for an interview with the head of the Government, and to communicate to him the exact state of the case.

On the 26th September, 1834, Mr. Babbage requested an audience of Lord Melbourne, for the purpose of placing these views before him; his Lordship acceded to the request, but from some cause the interview was postponed; and soon after, the ministry went out of office, without the desired conference having taken place.

The duration of the Duke of Wellington's administration was short; and no decision on the subject of the *Difference*-Engine was obtained.

In May, 1835, Mr. Babbage announced in a letter [17] to M. Quetelet, which was laid before the Academy of Sciences at Brussels, that he had " for six months been engaged in making the drawings of a new calculating engine of *far greater power than the first.*"   " I am myself astonished," says Mr. Babbage, " at the power I have been enabled to give to this machine; a year ago I should not have believed this result possible. This machine is intended to contain a hundred variables, or numbers susceptible of changing, and each of these numbers may consist of twenty-five figures.   The greatest difficulties of the invention have already been surmounted, and the plans will be finished in a few months."

Subsequently to the date of this letter, Mr. Babbage visited Turin, where he explained to Baron Plana, M. Menabrea, and several other distinguished philosophers of that city, the mathematical principles of his Analytical-Engine, and also the drawings and engravings of the more curious mechanical contrivances, by which those principles were to be carried into effect.   M. Menabrea, with Mr. Babbage's consent, published the information which he had received in the 41st volume of the *Bibliothèque Universelle de Génève.*   The article is remarkable as giving the first account of the Analytical-Engine.[18]   An English translation, with copious ori-

---

[17] Mr. Babbage informs me, that this letter was intended only as a private comunication.

[18] In the *Ninth Bridgewater Treatise,* Mr. Babbage has employed various arguments deduced from the Analytical-Engine, which afford some idea of its powers.   See second edition.   In 1838, several copies of plans of this new engine, engraved on wood, were circulated amongst Mr. Babbage's friends at the Meeting of the British Association at Newcastle.

In 1840, Mr. Babbage had one of his general plans of the Analytical-Engine lithographed at Paris.

ginal notes, made by a lady of distinguished rank and talent,[19] was published in the third volume of Taylor's *Scientific Memoirs.*

But it did not contain all the information respecting the Difference-Engine that was desirable, and Mr. Babbage was consequently led to communicate a short article upon this subject to the *Philosophical Magazine,* which is inserted in the 23rd volume[20]. The more comprehensive statements and official documents which Mr. Babbage has placed at my disposal renders it unnecessary to do more than allude to that article.

For nine years, that is, from the year 1833, when the construction of the Difference-Engine was suspended, until 1842, no decision respecting the machine was arrived at, although Mr. Babbage made several applications to Government on the subject.

On the 21st October, 1838, he wrote to the Chancellor of the Exchequer, stating that the question he wished to have settled was:—" Whether the Government required him to superintend the completion of the Difference-Engine, which had been suspended during

---

[19] I am authorized by Lord Lovelace to say, that the translator is Lady Lovelace.

[20] " The Difference-Engine could only tabulate, and was incapable by its nature of developing; the Analytical-Engine was intended to either tabulate or develop." The Difference-Engine is the embodying of one particular and very limited set of operations, the Analytical-Engine, the embodying of the science of operations. The distinctive characteristic of the Analytical-Engine, is the introduction into it of the principle which Jacquard devised for regulating by means of punched cards the most complicated patterns in the fabrication of brocaded stuffs. Nothing of the sort exists in the Difference-Engine. We may say most aptly, that the Analytical-Engine weaves *Algebraical patterns,* just as the Jacquard loom weaves flowers and leaves !"—Note to translation of Menabrea's Memoir. The 59th volume of the *Edinburgh Review* contains an able and elaborate article upon the Difference-Engine, written by Dr. Lardner.

the last five years, according to the original plan and principle, or whether they intended to discontinue it altogether." This letter produced no result. Time wore on, and Sir Robert Peel became Prime Minister. This was in 1841. Up to the termination of the Parliamentary Session in 1842, Mr. Babbage had received no other communication on the subject than a note from Sir George Clerk (Secretary to the Treasury), written in January of that year, stating that he feared the pressing official duties of Sir Robert Peel would prevent him turning his attention to the matter for some days.

Having availed himself of several private channels for recalling the question to Sir Robert Peel's attention without effect, Mr. Babbage, on the 8th of October, 1842, again wrote to him, requesting an early decision.

At last Mr. Babbage received the following letter:—

                    " *Downing Street, Nov.* 3, 1842.

" MY DEAR SIR,

                " The Solicitor-General has informed me that you are most anxious to have an early and decided answer as to the determination of the Government with respect to the completion of your Calculating Engine. I accordingly took the earliest opportunity of communicating with Sir R. Peel on the subject.

" We both regret the necessity of abandoning the completion of a Machine on which so much scientific ingenuity and labour have been bestowed. But on the other hand, the expense which would be necessary in order to render it either satisfactory to yourself, or generally useful, appears on the lowest calculation so far to exceed what we should be justified in incurring, that we consider ourselves as having no other alternative.

" We trust that by withdrawing all claim on the part of the Government to the Machine as at present constructed, and by placing it at your entire disposal, we may, to a degree, assist your future exertions in the cause of science.

I am, &c.

" *Charles Babbage, Esq.*"   " Henry Goulburn.

" P.S. Sir R. Peel begs me to add, that as I have undertaken to express to you our joint opinion on this matter, he trusts you will excuse his not separately replying to the letter, which you addressed to him on the subject a short time since."

To this letter Mr. Babbage replied as follows:—

" Dorset Street, Nov. 6, 1842.

" My dear Sir,

" I beg to acknowledge the receipt of your letter of the 3rd of Nov., containing your own and Sir Robert Peel's decision respecting the Engine for calculating and printing mathematical tables by means of Differences, the construction of which has been suspended about eight years.

" You inform me that both regret the necessity of abandoning the completion of the Engine, but that not feeling justified in incurring the large expense which it may probably require, you have no other alternative.

" You also offer, on the part of Government, to withdraw all claim in the Machine as at present constructed, and to place it at my entire disposal, with the view of assisting my future exertions in the cause of science.

" The drawings and the parts of the Machine already executed are, as you are aware, the absolute property of Government, and I have no claim whatever to them.

" Whilst I thank you for the feeling which that offer manifests, I must, under all the circumstances, decline accepting it.

" I am, &c.

" C. Babbage."

Mr. Babbage had an interview with Sir R. Peel subsequently to the date of the foregoing letter: the result was, however, entirely unsatisfactory ; and thus, with the communication from the then Chancellor of the Exchequer, terminated an engagement which had existed upwards of twenty years, during which period it is due to Mr. Babbage to state, that he refused more than one highly desirable and profitable situation[21], in order that he might give his whole time and thoughts to the fulfilment of the contract, which he considered himself to have entered into with the Government.

With respect to the Difference-Engine little remains to be added. In 1843, an application was made to Government, by the Trustees of King's College, London, to allow the Engine, as it existed, to be removed to the museum of that institution. The request was complied with ; and the Engine, enclosed within a glass case, now stands nearly in the centre of the Museum. It is capable of calculating to five figures, and two orders of differences, and performs the work with absolute precision ; but no portion whatever of printing machinery, which was one of the great objects in the construction of the Engine, exists. All the drawings of the machinery and other contrivances are also in King's College.

Before closing this Chapter, it will not be out of place to put upon record the state of the Analytical-Engine at this period (1848).

Mechanical Notations have been made, both of the actions of detached parts, and of the general action of the whole, which cover about four or five hundred large folio sheets of paper.

The original rough sketches are contained in about

---

[21] Mr. Babbage has shown me letters by which it appears that he declined offices of great emolument, the acceptance of which would have interfered with his labours upon the Difference-Engine.

five volumes.   There are upwards of one hundred large
drawings.   No part of the construction of the Analytical-Engine has yet been commenced.   A long series of
experiments have, however, been made upon the art of
shaping metals; and the tools to be employed for that
purpose have been discussed, and many drawings of
them prepared.   The great object of these inquiries
and experiments is, on the one hand, by simplifying the
construction as much as possible, and on the other, by
contriving new and cheaper means of execution, ultimately to reduce the expense within those limits which
a private individual may command.

THE annexed Review of the Eleventh Chapter of MR. WELD's HISTORY of the ROYAL SOCIETY, by Professor DE MORGAN, has been reprinted with his permission, and that of the Editor, *verbatim*, from the Athenæum of October 14th, 1848.

Three Notes at the foot of the pages have been added for the purpose of explanation.

These are followed by the remarks upon them, reprinted from the "*Athenæum*" of 16th December, 1848.

PROFESSOR DE MORGAN'S REVIEW *of* WELD'S
HISTORY *of the* ROYAL SOCIETY.

THE ATHENÆUM.
LONDON, SATURDAY, OCTOBER 14, 1848.

MR. BABBAGE'S CALCULATING MACHINE.

IN our review of Mr. Weld's "History of the Royal
Society," [*ante*, p. 621,] we noted that one chapter was
devoted to the history of the celebrated undertaking
above named. This chapter is taken from materials
furnished by Mr. Babbage himself, all the documents
having undergone the inspection of Mr. Weld. Of
recent publications on the subject it may be well to
note—1. A short account of the transactions with the
Government, communicated by Mr. Babbage to the
Philosophical Magazine for September, 1843. 2. A
sketch of the *Analytical Engine* (on which Mr. Babbage
is now at work, that commenced by the Government
being the *Difference Engine*) written in Italian by
Menabrea, and translated, with notes (and a list of all
previous publications), by the Countess of Lovelace
(August 1843). The statements put forward by Mr.
Babbage have thus been in substance before the public
for five years, without contradiction : for though the
account (No. 1) was not signed, it was stated to be
from authority, allowed to pass as such by the Editors

of the magazine, and generally understood to emanate from Mr. Babbage. We are then bound to take this first statement as admitted by Government, more especially after the publication by Mr. Weld, avowedly made from the documents furnished by Mr. Babbage himself: and assuredly we understand Mr. Weld as conceiving himself to be distinctly informed by Mr. Babbage, that *all* documents of any importance had been communicated.

The heads of the public history of the *Difference Engine* are as follows:—In April, 1823, the Government requested the opinion of the Royal Society on Mr. Babbage's plan for " applying machinery to the purposes of calculating and printing mathematical tables." The Royal Society reported favourably, that the machine was " fully adequate to the objects proposed,"—and this report was laid before Parliament. In July, Mr. Babbage had an interview with the Chancellor of the Exchequer (Earl of Ripon) to ascertain if Government would wish him to construct for *printing* as well as *calculating*. There is no minute of this conversation, and the parties have different memories upon it. But soon after, the Treasury informs the Royal Society that 1,500*l.* was to be issued to Mr. Babbage " to enable him to bring his invention to perfection, in the manner recommended." Mr. Weld remarks that no plan had been pointed out ; but it must be noticed that the original application was for an opinion upon *calculating and printing*, that the opinion spoke of the *full adequacy* of the plan for *the objects proposed*, and that the final determination of the Government was to proceed *as recommended.* Unless there were a previous understanding that all documents should either speak with the verbal completeness of an indictment or be wholly void, it is clear that the Government determined to assist Mr Babbage in realizing the full invention, and told him so.[1]

The work went on for four years, under advances of money from time to time: the funds were applied by Mr. Babbage, and the accounts were audited by Messrs. Brunel, Donkin, and Field. We suppose that Government did not exceed the proposed advance of 1,500l.; but this is not expressly stated. In December, 1828, Government applied again to the Royal Society to report upon the state, progress, and prospects of the machine. Mr. Babbage at the same time stated that he had expended 6,000l.—meaning we suppose, 4,500l. over and above the Government advance. A Committee, consisting of Messrs. Gilbert, Roget, Sabine, Herschel, Baily, Brunel (the elder), Kater, Donkin, Penn, Rennie, Barton, Warburton, declined to report on practicability or utility, considering both as fully established, and reported that, the difficulties considered, the progress was as great as could be expected, and that the engine was likely to fulfil the expectations of its inventor. On this report the Government made further advances, and the machine was declared national property. But the official payments soon failed: and Mr. Babbage called a meeting of private friends, in May 1829, who, on the representation that he had then advanced 4,000l. himself, in addition to the Government advance of 3,000l., advised him strongly not to proceed without adequate help from the Government.

---

[1] By the words "*no plan*," the reviewer here evidently refers to the *mechanical and mathematical plan*, on the fitness of which the Royal Society had already, as he observes, made a report. Mr. Weld, on the other hand, refers to the *mutual relations* of the two parties, Mr. Babbage and the Chancellor of the Exchequer, relative to the expenses and even to the ownership of the *Difference-Engine*, as appears by the footnote (7) at page 256.   C. B.

On this representation, the Duke of Wellington, Mr. Goulburn, and Lord Ashley inspected what there was to show, and the Treasury advanced 3,000*l.* more. In December 1830, nearly 600*l.* was still due to Mr. Babbage, " upon the last account," and that sum to the superintendent, Mr. Clement. The Treasury gave directions for the advance of 600*l.* to pay Mr. Clement, and desired a fresh inspection and opinion from the Royal Society. The Committee above named (with the addition of Sir J. Lubbock and Mr. Troughton) reported (April 1831) as favourably as before on every point, and recommended attention to Mr. Babbage's suggestion that the workshops should be removed to the neighbourhood of his residence. With regard to probable expense, they subjoined Mr. Brunel's estimate that 8,000*l.* additional would be sufficient; but recommending that the Government be advised to provide for 12,000*l.* by way of estimate. A piece of ground adjoining Mr. Babbage's garden was taken, and a fireproof building was erected. When about 17,000*l.* had been expended altogether, further progress was arrested by the extravagant demands made by Mr. Clement, as compensation for carrying on the construction in the new buildings. These were out of the question : and Mr. Clement withdrew, taking with him all the tools which had been used, many of which had been invented for the occasion. For it is the law that engineers and mechanics possess the right of property in all tools they have constructed, even though the cost of construction may have been defrayed by their employers. A special agreement ought, the reader will say, to have been made as to these tools; but whether the neglect is to be charged on Mr. Babbage, or on the Government, those must say who feel able. As it very seldom happens that the employer furnishes tools, it is easy to see how the necessity for a special agreement may have escaped the notice of all parties.

So far all is intelligible enough, and no blame attaches to either side, at least that we can venture to impute. But now the question divides in a curious way. While the works were suspended, Mr. Babbage reconsidered the whole question, and invented what he calls the *Analytical Engine,*—which we will take, on his word and Menabrea's publication, derived from his communications, to be immensely superior to the *Difference Engine.* To resume the latter, while Government was unacquainted with these new and more simple conceptions, would have been improper; to write on unfinished speculations would have been difficult. Mr. Babbage therefore (September 1834) requested a personal interview with Lord Melbourne; which was agreed to,—but before it took place the ministry was dissolved. From this time until 1842 Mr. Babbage made applications to the various administrations, which remained unanswered; until at last, in November, 1842, a letter from Mr. Goulburn, in answer to a new application, informed Mr. Babbage that the Government intended to discontinue the project on the ground of expense.

In the meanwhile Mr. Babbage incurred severe censure in scientific circles, as being himself the cause of the delay. It was asserted that he had compromised the Royal Society, which had so strongly recommended his project to the Government. It was pretty generally believed that the delay arose from his determination that the Government should take up the new engine and abandon the old one.

But, until the statement made by him shall be proved either false or defective, it must stand that the Government never returned any answer to the question—Shall the new engine be constructed, or shall the old one be proceeded with ?   We are of opinion that they ought to have required him to proceed with the old one. They ought to have said—The public can only judge by results : how well satisfied soever men of science may be that the new machine is immeasurably superior to the old one, society at large will never comprehend the abandonment of a scheme on which so much has been expended; they will say—What if, in constructing No. 2, No. 3 should be discovered, as much superior to No. 2 as No. 2 is to No. 1 !   And if Mr. Babbage had declined to proceed with his first project, when thus urged, it is our opinion that he would have richly deserved a very harsh censure.   And of this we are sure, that if Government had allowed him to finish the first machine, and he had done so with success, the House of Commons would willingly have granted money for the second,—aye, and for the third and fourth, if he had invented them.   But the Government itself prevented the matter from coming to any such issue.   It is possible that Sir R. Peel and Mr. Goulburn allowed Mr. Babbage's well-known wish[1] to abandon the first plan in favour of the new one to influence their decision. It may be that they were startled at finding that 17,000$l.$ expended upon one project was only the precursor of another.   If so, we think they put themselves in the wrong by not fastening on Mr. Babbage the alternative of either proceeding with the existing construction, or taking the entire responsibility of refusal upon himself.   As the matter now stands, and unless Mr. Babbage can be refuted, the answer to the question why he did not proceed is, that during the

---

[1] It is scarcely possible that this *supposed* wish could have influenced Sir Robert Peel, because he had before him a written disavowal of it from Mr. Babbage himself.   C. B.

eight years in which he had to bear the blame of the delay he could not procure even the attention of the Government, much less any decision on the course to be taken.

It is generally understood that Mr. Babbage is determined to proceed with the *Analytical Engine*, gradually, and at his own expense; and that the drawings are in a state of great forwardness. According to Mr. Babbage himself, many experiments have been made with the object " on the one hand, by simplifying " the construction as much as possible, and on the " other, by contriving new and cheaper means of execu- " tion, ultimately to reduce the expense within those " limits which a private individual may command."

In looking at all the circumstances of this statement, we regret its divided responsibility. Mr. Weld has seen Mr. Babbage's documents. Should he have made an insufficient selection, who is to blame? Mr. Weld says, " I have derived very valuable information from " an unpublished statement drawn up by Mr. Babbage, " which he has been so kind as to place in my hands. " The original documents, which are in Mr. Babbage's " possession, and which are referred to, I have myself " examined." From all this we should conclude that if Mr. Weld had omitted anything material, or fallen into any misconception, Mr. Babbage would before this have set it right. But it would be more satisfactory if we had Mr. Babbage's own acceptance of the statement thus made, as being that on which he is content to rest his case; at least until some specific counter-statement should demand more detail of explanation. Continued silence will be tantamount to such acceptance.

There is also one piece of information which must be drawn out before the case can be finally adjudicated. We stand thus:—Scientific rumour states that Mr.

Babbage compelled the Government to give him up by demanding permission to abandon the *Difference Engine* and substitute the *Analytical Engine*. To this, in the formal point of view, Mr. Babbage has fully answered, by showing that the Government never communicated to him that it was their pleasure he should proceed on the plan originally contemplated. The question now remains—Did Mr. Babbage, or did he not, in the several unanswered applications which he made to the Ministry, press the claims of the new machine and the abandonment of the old? If so, did he do it in such a manner as to give to understand, or make apparent, that he would not consent to recommence operations at the point of relinquishment? The "several applications" which were made from 1833 to 1838 are not particularized, much less described as to contents. But, in October 1838, Mr. Babbage wrote to the Chancellor of the Exchequer, stating, to use Mr. Weld's words, that "the question he wished to have settled" was, whether the Government required him to superintend the completion of the *Difference Engine* according to the original plan and principle, or whether they intended to discontinue it altogether. Now the words *quoted* are very like the idiom a person would employ who had in his mind that up to that time some other question had been among those proposed for discussion. And it is worthy of note that all the communications are un-described until we come to the one of October 1838; which shows that then at least, whether before or not, Mr. Babbage had put the question on the right issue. Of what tenor, then, were the undescribed applications?[1] If of the same as that of October 1838, Mr. Babbage stands quite clear; but if they were such as

---

[1] The two following will sufficiently explain them :—On the 23d December, 1834, Mr. Babbage addressed a statement to the Duke of

fairly to give rise to the rumour above mentioned, then it must be said, that though *he* had every disposition to get wrong, Government always prevented him by blocking his path with an error of its own. But in any case it is to be remembered, that for the last four years of unanswered application Mr. Babbage stood upon the right ground; and also that the rumoured *refusal* to proceed never was made.

The public, we think, has a right to explanation from the Government, and to further explanation from Mr. Babbage. Sir R. Peel turned it off with a joke in the House of Commons. He recommended that the machine should be set to calculate the time at which it would be of use. He ought rather to have advised that it should be set to compute the number of applications which might remain unanswered before a Minister, if the subject were not one which might affect his parliamentary power. If it had done this, it would have shown that its usefulness had commenced.

Wellington, pointing out the only plans which, in his opinion, could be pursued for terminating the questions relative to the *Difference Engine*, namely:

First, the Government might desire Mr. Babbage to continue the construction of the Engine in the hands of the person who has hitherto been employed in making it.

Secondly, the Government might wish to know whether any other person could be substituted for the engineer at present employed to continue the construction; a course which was possible.

Thirdly, the Government might (although he did not presume that they would) substitute some person to superintend the completion of the Engine instead of Mr. Babbage himself.

Fourthly, the Government might be disposed to give up the undertaking entirely.

A letter to Sir R. Peel from Mr. Babbage, dated 7th April, 1835, and enclosing the above plans, concludes thus:—

" The delays and difficulties of years will, I hope, excuse my expressing a wish that I may at length be relieved from them by an early decision of the Government on the question."   C. B.

MR. BABBAGE has reprinted, for private circulation, Mr. Weld's chapter on his *Calculating Machine*, and has appended to it our review[1] of that chapter [see *ante*, p. 1029] with three short foot-notes. The first of these is on a point immaterial to the issue; the second and third contain distinct statements of fact from Mr. Babbage, in reference to our comments upon his proceedings and those of the Government. Our readers will remember that from September 1834 to November 1842, Mr. Babbage could not procure the attention of the Government to the state of the engine, on which 17,000*l.* had been spent; and that, about the beginning of that period, Mr. Babbage had invented the new engine, which he called the *Analytical Engine.* And further, they will remember that all notion of the possibility of blame having been justly incurred by Mr. Babbage rested, in our comment, upon the hypothesis that he had put his wish to abandon the *Difference Engine* and substitute the *Analytical Engine* before the Government in such a form as to give them a right to suppose that he was unwilling to proceed with the former. On our remark that it is possible that Sir R. Peel and Mr. Goulburn allowed his well-known wish to influence their decision, Mr. Babbage observes :—
" It is scarcely possible that this *supposed* wish could

---

[1] We said in that review that Menabrea's Memoir was in Italian :— we should have said French.

" have influenced Sir Robert Peel, because he had
" before him a written disavowal of it from Mr. Bab-
" bage himself."

Again, of the first half of the period of unanswered
application Mr. Weld gives no account, as to the tenor
of the applications therein made to the Government:
though he shows by documents that during the second
half Mr. Babbage, to repeat our own phrase, " stood
upon the right ground." And thereupon we expressed
our opinion that the public had a right to explanation
from the Government, and to further explanation from
Mr. Babbage. This further explanation Mr. Babbage
now gives, in the following words; among which we
insert some bracketed comments:—

" The two following [applications made to the Govern-
" ment] will sufficiently explain them [the undescribed
" applications of the first half of the period of unan-
" swered application]:—On the 23rd December, 1834,
" Mr. Babbage addressed a statement to the Duke of
" Wellington, pointing out the only [the reader will
" remark this word *only*] plans which in his opinion
" could be pursued for terminating the questions rela-
" tive to the *Difference Engine*, namely—*First*, the
" Government might desire Mr. Babbage to continue
" the construction of the engine in the hands of the
" person who has hitherto been employed in making it.
" *Secondly*, the Government might wish to know whether
" any other person could be substituted for the engineer
" at present employed to continue the construction—a
" course which was possible. *Thirdly*, the Government
" might (although he did not presume that they would)
" substitute some person to superintend the completion
" of the engine instead of Mr. Babbage himself. *Fourthly*,
" the Government might be disposed to give up the
" undertaking entirely." A letter to Sir Robert Peel

from Mr. Babbage, dated the 7th of April, 1835, and enclosing the above plans, concludes thus: " The delays " and difficulties of years will, I hope, excuse my ex- " pressing a wish that I may at length be relieved from " them by an early decision of the Government on the " question."

From the above it appears that at the end of 1834, Mr. Babbage—though then so full of the *new* engine, that in September he had asked an audience of Lord Melbourne, to communicate the exact state of the case, and to request, of course, his consideration of the ques- tion whether the new engine should or should not take the place of the old one—began his applications to the Government with distinct reference to the *old* engine, and to the question of its completion or abandonment. Certainly the first of the two applications was not well timed, for it was made when the Duke of Wellington held all the seals, and a Government courier was hunt- ing Sir Robert Peel all over Italy, to tell him to come home quick and be Prime Minister.   But it was repeated to Sir Robert Peel in the April following, when the latter was also in official possession of the previous letter.

Mr. Babbage having thus filled up the only *lacuna* which the public press has brought to his notice, we can but repeat that those who would impute to him the blame of the failure of Government to complete his Calculating Machine must begin by proving his state- ment to be false or defective.   In 1835 he complains *to* the Government of " delays and difficulties," which he implies to be mainly caused *by* the Government, and he gets no answer whatever to repeated applications, until 1843.   Those who have propagated the rumours that his conduct was the cause of the delay, and that he compromised his friends in the Royal Society, who had aided in bringing him under the notice of the Government, are bound to abstain in future, or to show cause.

We end by a quotation from Mr. Weld, which we abstained from giving so long as we supposed that the discontinuance of the Calculating Machine might be, in any degree, Mr. Babbage's fault. " Mr. Babbage has shown me letters, by which it appears that he declined offices of great emolument, the acceptance of which would have interfered with his labours upon the *Difference Engine*."

THE END.

For EU product safety concerns, contact us at Calle de José Abascal, 56–1°, 28003 Madrid, Spain or eugpsr@cambridge.org.